High-Energy Teaching

High-Energy Teaching

by M. Walker Buckalew, Ph.D.

Published by

ism®

Independent School Management, Inc.

Wilmington, Delaware
1993

Printed in the United States of America.
Set in 10-point Stone Serif.

ISBN 1-883627-00-1

ism®

Independent School Management, Inc.
1316 North Union Street
Wilmington, DE 19806-2594
302/656-4944
FAX 302/656-0647

Acknowledgements

After the publication in 1992 of *Twenty Principles for Teaching Excellence,* I conducted summer and fall workshops for more than 600 teachers throughout the United States. Those teachers, being teachers, taught me something important.

They taught me that in addition to their considerable interest in, and eagerness to argue about, applications of the 20 Principles (and 35 Sub-principles) to their classrooms, they were even more eager to hear about and to discuss that book's *leitmotif*: teacher self-renewal. The more workshops I conducted during that time period, the more certain I became that *Teaching Excellence* needed a companion piece.

Teaching Excellence, those 600-plus teachers taught me, does do what it was designed to do. That is, it provides a research-based argument, in workbook form, that helps teachers develop approaches to eliciting consistently good student performance in classrooms at all grade levels. It suggests what to do.

This book, *High-Energy Teaching,* suggests not so much "what to do" as "HOW TO BE."

If you've already read *Teaching Excellence,* you may have grown a little thoughtful about its implications. How can a classroom professional like you approach teaching from such a high-intensity standpoint – and survive? Psychologically, motivationally, emotionally, physically, interpersonally. How does a human being engage that seriously in the process and come out of it in one piece?

That's the issue *High-Energy Teaching* is designed to help you with. If you've already read the other book, that's OK, of course. But I do think of this book as the "enabler" for the first one.

And that leads me to my first acknowledgement: To those 600-plus teachers who helped me see last summer and fall that another installment was needed, thank you. I got the message.

Secondly, I want to thank the four practicing teachers who read this entire manuscript during a mere four weeks of what must certainly have been solidly booked teaching time during spring of 1993: Carl I. Denlinger, Donna Hillenbrand, Kathleen O'Brien, and Jan Miles Odom.

Thank you. You helped immensely in refining *High-Energy Teaching* so that your colleagues would have the clearest, most readable volume possible.

Finally, my thanks go to the nine staff members who form the "CTR Team" here at our ISM Center for Teacher Renewal: Roxanne Elliott, Terri Gillespie, Marguerite Goff, Becca Hutchinson, Jane Koester, Janet Powers, Kelly Rawlings, Pat Stopa, and Terri Tackett. That list includes executives, researchers, marketers, writers, and editors.

But for this project, we were without labels. We were, plainly and simply, a team. Thank you.

Walker Buckalew

Wilmington, Delaware

May 1993

Dedicated to my own Prime Movers –

Mrs. Marsh (3rd grade)

Mrs. Blakemore (5th grade)

Mrs. Reich (high school)

Mr. Tandy (high school)

Dr. White (college)

Contents

Section I:
Explanation

Chapter 1

Pudding and Prime Movers

I have always been interested to discover, when on-site at any school, which members of the school's teaching staff are regarded – and by whom – as Prime Movers. Simply put, Prime Movers are those who are known to provide students with "the big push."

Prime Movers can be hard for the visitor, or even colleagues, to ferret out. Their power to move kids off dead center and onto a new track is obvious sometimes only to students themselves. Because Prime Movers are almost always excellent teachers, by any definition, their "prime mover-hood" eventually becomes known to others: parents, alumni, the administration, the faculty. Prime Movers themselves may or may not be comfortable acknowledging their power. But it is obviously there to those who study under them.

For this book's purposes, the crucial thing about Prime Movers is that they tend to stay highly *renewed,* day in and day out, year after year.

Think about yourself. How many students, alumni, colleagues, administrators, parents of students, and so on, would name you as a Prime Mover?

Thousands? Hundreds? Several dozen? Six? Two? One? Or none?

What I want to propose for your consideration is this: The more likely people are to regard you as a Prime Mover, the more likely you are to be highly self-renewing, maintain high levels of performance, maintain high levels of health, and maintain "managed" levels of stress in your professional life.

Unfortunately, for most teachers the school environment is just not set up to enhance your continued renewal, or to be a moderate-stress, healthy situation. You're so busy grading papers, planning class lessons, and enforcing rules, not to mention the whirlwind of your personal life outside the classroom, that you don't have time to concentrate on your own professional progress – achievements as well as weak points – or your ability to perform well every day in that kind of stressful setting.

But I'm not here to dwell on the negative. Through research findings I will share with you, I have found there are methods that you – all by yourself – can use to self-renew, both professionally and personally, by enhancing your performance, maintaining high levels of health, and shaping stress. You owe it to yourself and your chosen vocation to nurture the original commitment you made to teaching. With a Professional Development Plan you'll customize in Section II to fit your needs and purposes, and with the stress-shaping, health- and performance-enhancing tools I will explain in Section III, you, too, can sustain levels of excellence characteristic of the finest Prime Movers. After one year, 12 years, even 36 years as a teacher, you can increase your excitement for your profession – and become a more effective, satisfied professional at the same time.

The Pudding

The proof is in the pudding. One of my own Prime Movers (Mrs. Marsh, third grade, Cascade Heights Elementary) used to say that a lot.

The proof, she drummed into our heads, is in the pudding. If you, as a professional, are highly self-renewing, you probably go to work most Monday mornings with some sense of excitement. And you look forward to the next school year, when you'll be able to apply some of the good ideas you developed this year. You imagine yourself teaching five or 10 years from now, and you like what you imagine. It all strikes you as personally stimulating and rewarding, quite aside from, and in addition to, what the students will get from their experiences with you.

To give yourself a good chance to live the highly self-renewing experience I describe, please entertain the idea that the following ideas are true – or could be true, if you choose to operate in the ways implied by them:

- teaching is leadership;
- teaching is knowledge;
- teaching is relationships;
- teaching is NOT a technocratic activity;
- teaching is NOT a management activity;
- teaching is NOT – and should not be allowed to become – an efficient activity.

This list may go down hard with some of you.

Bear with me. I can make this palatable.

I know you've learned a certain way to look at teaching and your role in it, and you're comfortable in that. I don't want to know if you're comfortable, though; I want to know if you experience continual renewal in your professional commitment. I want to know if you're intellectually and emotionally stimulated by what you're doing. I want to know if you're moving yourself, and therefore your students, and therefore our society toward rejuvenation and regeneration.

A Seminal Experience

More than a quarter century ago, three weeks into my first official, paid teaching position, I was jolted by a completely unexpected personal/professional experience. That experience gave me a hint, early on, that this career could be powerfully renewing, if the conditions were right, and if my own mind-set and emotion-set were right.

It was during the mid-'60s. Racial integration was upon the public schools in some parts of the country. Having already had experience in interracial leadership of young people, I volunteered to teach English, math, and public speaking at a high school that had a 100 percent African-American student body and, prior to my arrival, a 100 percent African-American faculty and staff.

As I was also an assistant football coach, my work with a portion of the student body began more than two weeks before school started. When school did start, it began with two half-days. Then, on the first full day, a pep rally was held during the last period. The entire student body, faculty, and staff assembled in the gymnasium.

Cheerleaders cheered. The principal spoke. The band played. The students shouted. And, finally, the head coach made his remarks and, one by one, introduced the assistant coaches.

My two assistant coaching colleagues and I were seated with our classes. The two of them were introduced first. Warm applause followed each introduction.

Then I was introduced. As with my colleagues, applause followed, then diminished. As my colleagues had, I stood to acknowledge the applause, and, as it waned, I sat down.

Then something odd happened. I sensed that the applause was swelling again. Looking to my left, I saw that all the members of the 55-man football team had climbed to their feet, had turned to face me, and were applauding *at me*.

I stared at them, amazed.

Then, recovering, I stood to acknowledge the gesture. Their applause continued. Growing uncomfortable, I waved gratefully to them and sat down.

Teaching is leadership.

Teaching is knowledge.

Teaching is relationships.

For years, I felt there was something generalizable rooted in that experience, but I was not sure what it was. Certainly, the racial uniqueness of the situation and of that era itself played its part and accounted for the team's gesture.

But I, novice though I was, had done something right, too. I had done something that allowed the racial uniqueness of the situation to generate a powerful, unforgettable experience for me as a young teacher.

I really did not know what I had done, nor could I analyze what had happened.

I do know now, however, and I understand how to analyze the event. The variables are indeed universal, and they are the same variables that link so strongly with teacher self-renewal. They are the variables that lead us to conceive of teaching as "leadership, knowledge, and relationships."

What distinguished me, as a young coach, from me, as a young English/math/public speaking teacher, was my intuitive application on the field, and lack of application in the classroom, of those leadership, knowledge, and relationships maxims.

In my classroom – and not just in my first year, and not just at my first school – I privately bemoaned the lack of enthusiasm so evident in the kids as they entered each day, each period. In my mind, I contrasted that with the eagerness with which they took the field or the court.

It did not occur to me that their demeanor mirrored my own.

Of course, you are ahead of me. You figured that out long ago. You've understood for a long time that many students – of any age – could be infused with enthusiasm if only they sensed it in you, their potential Prime Mover.

Even if I had understood any of that, nothing would have happened. That mind-set and emotion-set required something I was not ready to give. It required that I personally display, first, an obvious commitment to, and excitement about, the academic and other teaching/learning challenges we sought to confront each day in the classroom, and second, a willingness to draw from myself the same kind of passion I displayed when coaching. Not the same *behaviors*. The same *passion*.

The members of that football team saluted me because I was assertive with them on the field (teaching is leadership), because I knew what I was doing on the field (teaching is knowledge), and, above all, because I was immersed with them in the endeavor (teaching is relationships). The racial conditions heightened their sense – and mine – of that third factor.

Several years later, I accepted a middle-school teaching position in

English and social studies, a position with no coaching or other extra-curricular leadership activities. I resigned after six weeks. Given my mind-set and emotion-set, there was no self-renewal implicit in that situation, and *I did not know how to create it.*

Although the principal seemed to think things were fine, I was bored. The kids were bored. It was intolerable. This is not the natural condition of professional organizational life. None of us should merely try to "get used to it."

And that is the point. Educationally, I was right to resign. If we – you and I – cannot approach the teaching enterprise in ways that literally fill us with excitement, mutual teacher/student stimulation, and a sense of continuing renewal, then we owe it to ourselves, our families, our students, their parents, and our society, to quit.

Some of you should quit. Many more of you should not. You should, instead, reject the stultification you may have begun to experience. You should redesign your career to ensure its ongoing self-renewal.

Many of you figured all that out much earlier in your careers than I did. I just want to be sure you are conscious of this fact: *There can be no self-renewal without a regularly enhanced commitment to, and an immersion in, the lives of your students.* You cannot be renewed "from a distance." The renewal is in the pudding.

Chapter 2

Long Odds and the Big Picture

You cannot be renewed "from a distance."

The problem with that – with what I just wrote in Chapter 1 – is that, while maybe it's true (you're saying) that immersion is necessary for renewal, it's also true (you're thinking) that no one can immerse indefinitely. If we seriously attempt that, as teachers, we drown. We expire. We burn out. We experience exhaustion.

Teachers cannot maintain that level of commitment – that degree of passion – for very long.

Or can they?

The striking thing about teaching, when viewed from the vantage point of other professions, is that teachers are nearly always "on." Regardless of a given teacher's level of commitment, degree of passion, or extent of immersion, that teacher is "on" almost all the time.

There are few respites in the day, and those respites are almost never at times spontaneously chosen by the teacher. In other professions, an individual may say to the secretary, "I really need a break here. Hold the calls. I'm going for a walk." In teaching, that same, simple action would probably result in the teacher's dismissal. "What do you mean, you're going for a walk? You have 25 kids in front of you." (Or is it 35?)

You've seen those "occupational stress" research studies. Maybe you've been confused by the fact that, in some of them, teaching comes out mid-range, apparently a moderate-stress occupation; in other studies, teaching comes out near the top, apparently a very high-stress occupation. In at least one such study, teaching ranked second only to air traffic controlling on the stress scale.

So, which is it? Moderate stress or very high stress?

As you'd guess, that depends on the researcher's assumptions, and the researcher's measuring units. If the assumption is that stress is a function of the extent to which one has "perceived control" over his or her work environment, teaching comes out as a mid-range stressful occupation. People in countless other occupations would sacrifice a great deal, in fact, to be able to go into their own room, close the door, make plans unencumbered by a hovering boss, and conduct their business almost entirely unsupervised. High levels of perceived control translate into low-to-moderate stress, on most scales.

(Such studies, however, tend to ignore the extent to which a given teacher exercises successful organizational/behavioral control over the students; this part of the "perceived control" issue is usually not taken into account by this type of occupational survey.)

If, instead, the operational assumption underlying the occupational stress study is the extent to which the subjects are under unremitting pressure to perform, then teaching (and air traffic controlling) rise to the top of the heap. As I noted earlier, teachers are always "on."

Teachers cannot decide to take a break when class is in full swing any more than an air traffic controller can take a break when a Boeing 747 is on final approach. There is no "good time" to step away from responsibilities of this sort. While the classroom may not literally crash and burn while you're gone, it may do the instructional and behavioral equivalent.

To emphasize the fact that you have plenty of company, and to highlight the fact that in order to "shape your stress," you may have to scale some walls, I'd like you to read and compare the data from over a decade of research conducted by Dr. Milbrey McLaughlin.[1] More than 10 years ago, while a senior social scientist with the Rand Corporation,

---

1 Quotations from Dr. McLaughlin's remarks to the 1983 National Association of Independent Schools' (NAIS) annual conference, as summarized in the spring 1984 newsletter. Reprinted by permission of the National Association of Independent Schools.

McLaughlin began researching teacher-renewal issues at length. Through her research, she arrived at the following disturbing comments.

> The cellular organization of schools means that teachers are alone for most of their professional hours – physically and psychically apart from their colleagues and from professional support. Partly because of this isolation and partly because of teachers' practice or tradition of not sharing, there is little common "technical" culture in schools. Not only are the good things not shared; the bad things – the less successful practices – also go unnoticed and, by and large, unremarked upon. The absence of a professional culture is a major impediment to professional growth. When teachers do ask for help, assistance they rate more useful typically comes from fellow teachers and administrators, not from specialists, outside consultants, or university gurus. However, the normal course of events in a school day makes this kind of collegial assistance very difficult to acquire.

What do teachers care about? When asked what they care about – their greatest rewards, their greatest sources of pride – teachers pointed consistently to the success of students, both of individual students who have achieved something, and of groups of students who have moved or progressed. The second most frequent response teachers gave concerned the respect given to them by their colleagues. Both responses are rooted in professional incentives, for teachers care most about professionalism and about what brought them to teaching in the first place. Professionalism is foremost in determining how teachers view their working climate.

> A sense of uncertainty characterizes teachers and teaching, for teachers say they have difficulty in assessing their own effectiveness and evaluating their own work to such a degree that most see this as an obstacle to their own growth and development. The intangibility, complexity, and remoteness of the results of teaching/learning (and other influences) on students make it hard for teachers to determine what effect they have on their students. Ironically, this uncertainty, which teachers articulate clearly, undermines the very pride and satisfaction which they cite as a source of motivation. Teachers generally do not have time or support for individual or collective reflection on or analysis of what they are doing.
>
> Most teachers are unlikely to see or act on the need for change, whether it be change that they themselves identify or change that colleagues might identify for them. Yet research studies on planned

> change and teacher evaluation give clear evidence that, when interaction of this sort does occur, especially on a regular basis, it has a substantial, powerful, and positive effect on what and how well students learn.
>
> We also have powerful evidence that teaching does *NOT* become more rewarding as time passes. Without exception, those who have taught five years or more admit that they no longer feel the enthusiasm, excitement, recognition of their talents, and challenge they once did. They see no professional growth ahead and rarely experience a sense of personal or intellectual growth either. [*emphasis added*]
>
> The final point of agreement about the life of teachers concerns stress. ... Couched in terms of the relative stressfulness of occupations, teachers rank second only to air traffic controllers.

The Human Stress Response

Now let's take a look at what happens to you when you're under that kind of daily, hourly, by-the-minute stress. First let's examine research by Dr. Hans Selye on the mammalian stress response. In a typical experiment, Selye's team would place individual mice in a variety of stressful settings: a box too warm; a box too cold; a box too crowded; a box subjected to loud, unpredictable noises; a treadmill; a shock-avoidance environment. Upon sacrificing these small mammals, the team found that the same internal events were always evident – swollen adrenal gland, shrunken thymus, ulcerated stomach. There it was: the mammalian stress response.

It is no accident, Selye found, that people with serious illnesses, and whose bodies are therefore under immense stress, "look sick." Nor is it any accident that otherwise healthy people who select stressful occupations begin eventually to look "haggard," or "tired," or "run down," or "distracted," or "depressed." Common psychophysiological events are at work inside them.

Teachers fit this profile exactly.

How can a teacher find continual self-renewal through passionate, committed, continual immersion in the lives of the kids and not become haggard, tired, run down, distracted, depressed – the symptoms of persistent, long-term stress and early burn-out?

The Selye-Snelling Stress Curve

At first glance, Selye's General Adaptation Syndrome[2] appears only to make matters worse. Shown below, this "stress curve" displays the standard mammalian (including human) response to stress. The first stage (A), Selye termed the alarm stage; the second (B), the resistance stage; and the third (C), the exhaustion stage.

(In small-animal experiments, the exhaustion stage may end with the death of the creature; in teaching, one hopes that the teacher's symptoms – fatigue, mild depression, minor illness – lead to a response such as rest, relaxation, recuperation, resignation and/or retirement, and that these "safeguard" responses are brought into play long before such finality.)

The General Adaptation Syndrome

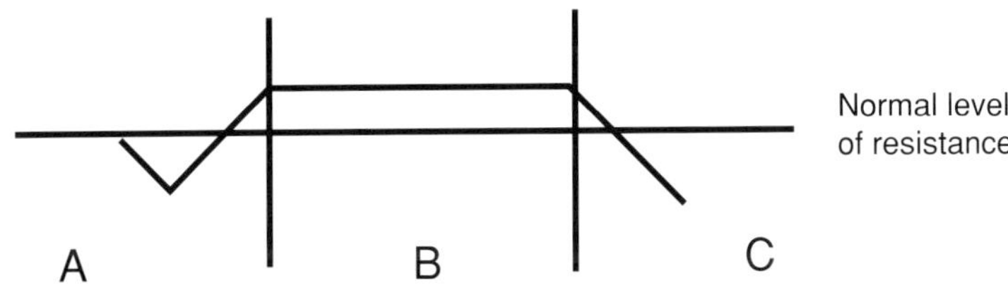

Seeing this General Adaptation Syndrome – the stress curve – presented by me in a workshop in the mid-'70s, veteran school leader and analyst Dr. W. Rodman Snelling hypothesized that something like the Selye stress curve might affect many schools on an annual, cyclical basis, and that the phenomenon might account for what he perceived to be deterioration in both teacher and student performance as the school year plodded through its interminable winter and spring months (regardless, incidentally, of climate and temperature).

2 Selye, Hans, *Stress without Distress*, New York: New American Library, 1974.

The second figure, shown below, shows the theoretical Selye-Snelling stress curve that resulted from that 1970s hypothesis.

The Selye-Snelling Stress Curve (hypothetical)

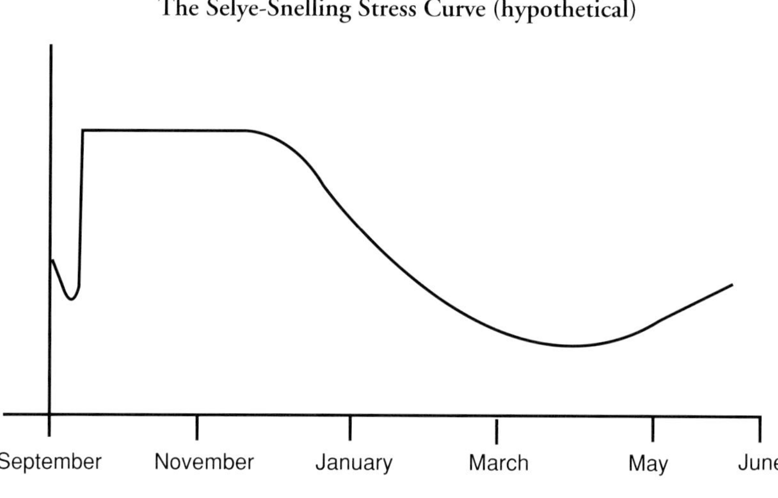

Hypothesized Faculty/Student Performance Levels

How does that strike you, intuitively? Does it seem consistent with what you think you see in your students? In yourself? In your colleagues?

And, above all, what do you answer to the questions I continue to ask in this text on your behalf?

- *Doesn't this make still clearer the impossibility of maintaining the sort of passionate, committed, all-out, high-energy immersion with kids just advocated in the first chapter?*
- *Doesn't this show emphatically that you cannot sustain that kind of effort for the duration of even a single school year, to say nothing of a career?*
- *Doesn't this make impossible this book's insistence that renewal must be sought in immersion with your students?*

The Center for Teacher Renewal: the Pilot Study

The Center for Teacher Renewal (CTR) pilot study – a descriptive study from The International Model Schools Project – has provided some interesting evidence in support of the fact that teachers can remain immersed in their students' lives and still have the energy to perform well, stay healthy, and continually renew their passion for their chosen vocation. Furthermore, you can do this yourself, without help from others.

The three figures on the following pages provide an overview. In structured interviews with 42 school leaders, interesting patterns emerged. Each of the three figures contrasts the 15 "best" (that is, most consistent) schools with the 15 "worst" (that is, least consistent) schools. Notice how, in these school leaders' estimates of their faculties' performance, enthusiasm, and stress, relatively narrow gaps between best and worst in the fall become much larger gaps as the school year progresses.[3]

This pilot study provided some evidence in support of a pessimistic view: deterioration in teacher performance and enthusiasm did seem apparent in many schools, and perceived teacher stress climbed in those schools as the year progressed, especially at year's end. But the study also provided some hope. In certain other schools, little deterioration occurred; performance and enthusiasm traced relatively straight lines, while stress remained much more stable and slightly more moderate.

So, the issue becomes, what were those "good" schools like?

The single most striking difference between the "good" and the "bad" was *esprit de corps* – or lack of it. In schools in which perceived faculty performance and enthusiasm started high and stayed high year-round, a "sense of community" existed and was carefully nurtured by the teachers and administrators. Teachers were more likely to be helpful to each other. Teacher conversations were less likely to be counterproductive complaint sessions and more likely to have problem-solving as the focus.

---

[3] The patterns shown by the "worst" schools' faculties' perceived performance/enthusiasm show remarkable similarity to those traced by students in a four-year case study of a single school, conducted by members of the Yale University sociology department in the early 1970s (Alderfer, C. P., & Brown, L. D., *Learning from Changing: Organizational Diagnosis and Development*, Beverly Hills and London: Sage Publications, 1975). For further discussion, see page 175.

Refer to this book's Appendix, as well, for a display of Pearson Product-Moment correlations used with these pilot study data. Note that the perceived "faculty stress" relationships were statistically non-significant. Teacher stress can apparently be reduced and "shaped"; it certainly does not go away.

The Center for Teacher Renewal: The Pilot Study

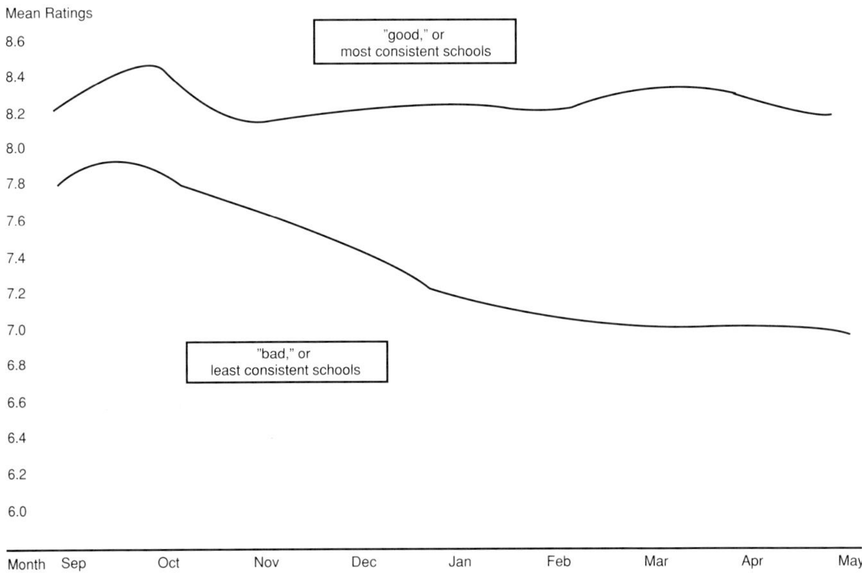

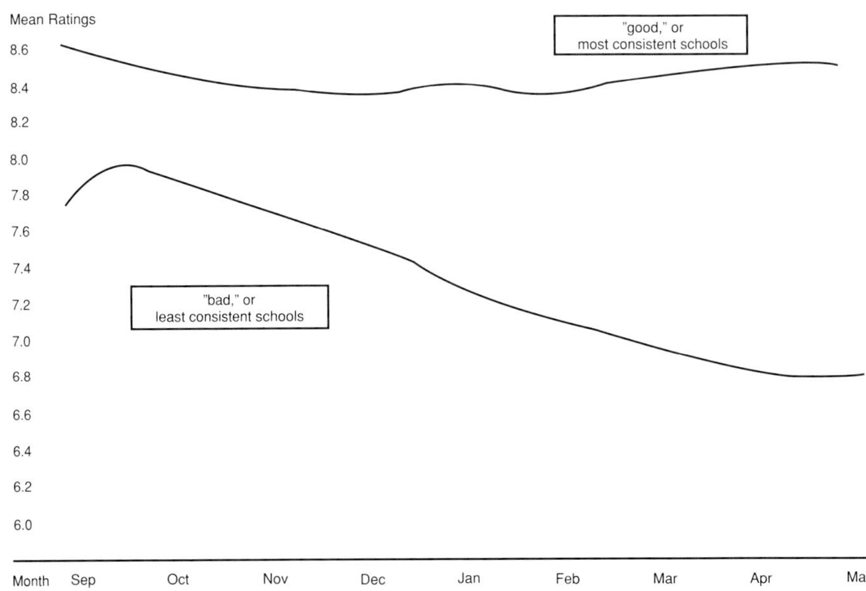

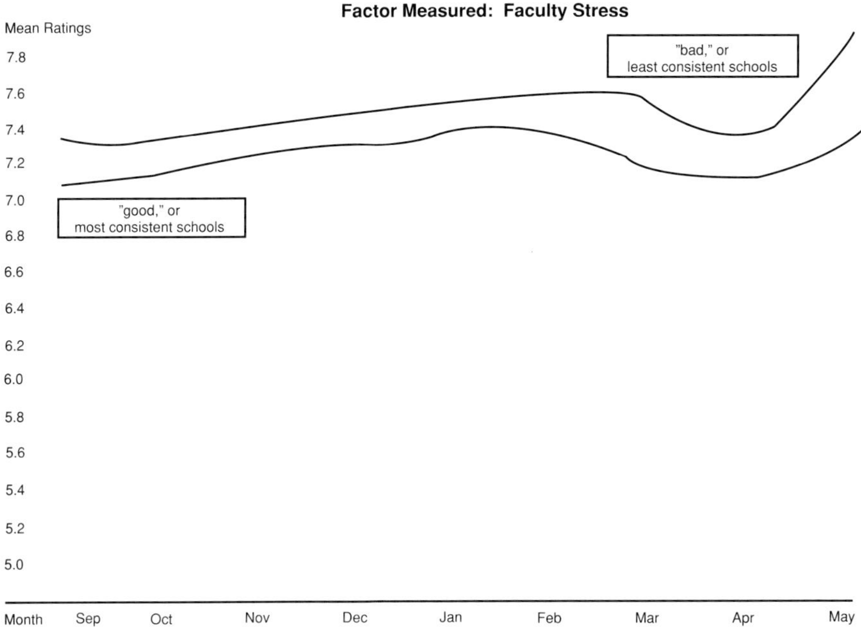

Some of this was organized through whole-group or small-group faculty meetings; some of it was spontaneous. Either way, it made *big* differences.

The teachers in the "good" schools, I should emphasize, were working extremely hard, probably harder than those in the other schools (though I can't support that with data). They appeared to be immersed with their students, showing the kind of commitment that I have talked about several times already in this book. But they stayed "up" year-round. They remained energized. Their perceived stress levels, while certainly not low, were nonetheless lower and more stable than those in other schools.

And there it is again. No renewal "from a distance." Instead, we find "renewal" and "immersion" hand-in-hand.

Fortunately, McLaughlin's recent research, under the aegis of the Consortium for Policy Research in Education, has exposed strategies that lead to teacher empowerment, and thereby increase teacher career satisfaction. The strategies from McLaughlin's recent research support similar research findings by the CTR, which have shown that "learned helplessness" occurs when teachers perceive that their efforts do not bring about desired results, and that the exact opposite phenomenon – "learned optimism" – occurs when teachers perceive that their efforts are rewarded with desired outcomes.[4]

According to McLaughlin's recent research on teacher empowerment strategies, there are two methods, in particular, from which teachers draw both power and career satisfaction. These are (1) knowledge of and interest in their discipline/subject area, and (2) knowledge of and participation in their professional community. The teachers McLaughlin studied who employed these two "teacher empowerment strategies" believed they were empowered in both principle and practice, felt a sense of both community and excitement in their teaching environments, and had attitudes about teaching that were upbeat, hopeful, and enthusiastic. What follows are excerpts from Dr. McLaughlin's 1991 research-based report on these two major factors of teacher empowerment.[5]

Teachers' knowledge, immersion, and interest in their disciplines may be the single most important factor in empowering teachers:

> Knowing a subject well entails knowing information about many topics in the discipline, having an awareness of connections between those topics, and demonstrating facility in the methods and ways of thinking commonly used within the discipline.
>
> Breadth and depth of disciplinary knowledge empowers teachers in three ways: it provides the foundation of their authority and thus their professional discretion, it provides a basis for involvement in a professional community, and it has direct relevance in school and/or district policy decisions.
>
> Broad and deep knowledge of subject matter improves daily decision-making in the classroom; it enables teachers to convey ideas in diverse and creative ways to their students. Disciplinary knowledge informs decisions about what and how to teach to best serve

---

4 See Chapter 4, page 50, for further discussion of Dr. Martin E. P. Seligman's concepts of "learned helplessness" and "learned optimism."

5 Lichtenstein, Mary; Mc Laughlin, Milbrey; and Knudsen, Jennifer, *Teacher Empowerment and Professional Knowledge*. Consortium for Policy Research in Education, 1991.

> student needs. In addition, disciplinary knowledge forges connections to a professional community of teachers and others who use [that same discipline].

Faculty collaboration and coalition in inter- and intra-school professional cultures is an effective strategy for combating the feeling of professional isolation that is pervasive in most classroom settings; such collaboration is second only to discipline knowledge in promoting teacher empowerment:

> Professional affiliation is helpful to teachers for solving immediate classroom problems; having access to such a strong base is empowering.
>
> Beyond the immediate practical value of these networks, teachers reconceptualize their roles and responsibilities as a result of their new affiliations, and they do so in ways that enhance their identification with the profession. Professional community empowers teachers in two ways. First, it helps them recognize their own expertise. Second, it expands teachers' notions of what is possible within their own practice and the profession as a whole.
>
> The safety, support, and stimulation provided by collaboration empowers teachers to extend themselves professionally because it validates their risk-taking [in a supportive and tolerant yet professionally critical] community.

Now, the caveat.

In these kinds of studies, nothing gets "proved." You can't wave this book around (or even its more academic-sounding Appendix) and claim you've found proof that teacher renewal is yours for the taking, just by bolstering your faculty's sense of community, its academic preparation, or its professional affiliation. You can wave this book around, of course. Just don't make the wrong claims for it.

Quite frankly, you may not be able to do much about your school's sense of community. But you *can* do something about the sense of community in your own classroom. And you *can* do something about improving your own performance, shaping stress, and maintaining your enthusiasm for teaching.

This book presents my ideas on these topics of renewal, performance, health, and stress. The ideas come from decades of doing research, from studying other people's research, from working with teachers and kids, from teaching in public schools and universities, from administrating in public schools and universities, and from trying to be thoughtful in all those contexts. Some of this book's ideas, as you would expect, are research-derived; others are experience-derived; others express, or are derived from, accepted facts and concepts in several academic fields (cognitive psychology, physiology, and sociology); still others are combinations of two or three of those disciplines.

As with anything you encounter, you'll read this material and think about it. If you're sufficiently intrigued, you'll actually do something with it. If the outcome of your efforts is a Professional Development Plan for yourself (see Chapter 3) – one that keeps you emotionally and intellectually stimulated for the long run – and a personal commitment to shape stress so that you're physically and psychologically able to meet the daily rigors of your profession, then my goal for this book will have been met.

Chapter 3

We're Talking About Your *Life* Here

So now (you're thinking), how exactly do I reconcile the difficulty of finding long-term teacher career satisfaction with the more hopeful notes sounded in the research on teacher empowerment and in the CTR's recent studies? To start, get a handle on this by rating yourself and your current classroom setting, using my questions from McLaughlin's list for a framework. Bear in mind as you complete the following questionnaire that this is not so much a rating of you, the professional, as it is a rating of your teaching context. Your goal is to determine the extent to which your context fits – or does not fit – with McLaughlin's list of research-derived characteristics.

And by the way, please understand that I'm assuming throughout this questionnaire and throughout *High-Energy Teaching* that you will be unable to answer "Yes" to many of these items, and maybe to none at all.

Degree of Isolation

1. I have a total of at least one hour's worth of *substantive*, solution-focused conversation with at least one colleague every week. Yes _____
2. I team-teach or co-teach with at least one colleague, for at least one class session, at least once every week. Yes _____
3. I have easy, comfortable access to at least one colleague for help with classroom problems, and actually use this access route regularly (at least twice a month). Yes _____

4. I have reliable means for learning about my colleagues' successful and unsuccessful practices (access to a "technical/professional culture"). Yes _____

5. Faculty (or division or department) meetings are held at least weekly, and provide opportunities to discuss – in professional, problem-focused and problem-solving terms – *substantive* instructional issues at some length (more than 20 minutes), in each instance. Yes _____

6. The faculty culture in my school is supportive – that is, I have plenty of evidence, readily and regularly apparent, that my colleagues value me for my efforts with our students. Yes _____

Success Criteria

1. I am provided with reliable data regarding my students' success or lack of success at the next levels of schooling (or in job settings, if that is the next step for some of them). Yes _____

2. It is realistically possible for me to collect information on my own about individual students' success at the next levels of schooling (or in job settings, where appropriate). Yes _____

3. I am able to assess *objectively and accurately* the progress that individual, and groups of, students make while under my tutelage each year (by means of, for example, pre- and post-tests systematically administered, or individualized software programs that electronically track student progress throughout the year). Yes _____

Long-term Professional Growth

1. My school (or system or district) encourages individual teachers to develop long-term professional growth plans, and then provides financial and other assistance in moving toward the planned goals. (This does not refer to graduate study or graduate degrees, though these could be included as elements in such a plan. This means, instead, planned movement toward intellectual, teaching-related fields of interest, toward teaching-technique skills acquisition, toward intellectual and/or skill-related "re-tooling" for predicted new frontiers in relevant teaching fields.) Yes _____

2. In the absence of any school (or system or district) support, it is real-

istically possible for me to develop and implement my own long-term professional growth plan, as just described. Yes _____

Time for Analysis and Reflection

1. For a total of at least 60 minutes a month, time is provided in my professional day for analysis of my teaching work, either aided by a colleague or alone (this does not refer to "planning periods"). Yes _____

2. For a total of at least 60 minutes a month, I create time for "Ritual Reflection" and *recommitment to my vocation*, and for reflection in that context on the quality and effectiveness of my teaching efforts. Yes _____

Stress Patterns and Levels – Psychological and Physiological

1. On an average of three days per week or more, year-round, I feel invigorated and fulfilled at the end of the school day. Yes _____

2. For well over half the total weeks in the school year, I find myself looking forward on Sunday evenings to Monday morning at school. Yes _____

3. Most of the time (four hours or more), on most days (three per week or more), throughout the school year, I find myself "lost in my work" – in the best sense of that phrase – *enjoying* the give-and-take of the teaching/learning experience, gratified by a "background" sense of doing meaningful service, and actually *happy* to be where I am. Yes ____

4. Most of the time (at least 15 out of every 20 working days, year-round) I am absolutely without stress symptoms (e.g., stomach problems, headaches, a heightened sense of anxiety, a feeling of malaise, mild depression, persistent fatigue). Yes _____

5. Most of the time (at least 15 out of every 20 working days, year-round) I am "even-tempered" in my classroom. (This implies that confrontations with students are reasoned, on the teacher's part, and not self-destructive to the teacher emotionally, psychologically, or physically; this does not imply a low frequency of confrontations.) Yes _____

6. As an indicator of my overall health and ability to perform, I know what my diastolic and systolic blood pressure readings are on a weekly basis, year-round. Yes _____
7. My diastolic blood pressure never exceeds 85. Yes _____
8. I know what my HDL and LDL cholesterol readings are, at my peak stress period(s) per school-year cycle (late spring for many teachers, according to the CTR pilot study). Yes _____
9. My HDL cholesterol reading, at my peak stress period(s), is at least 43 mg/dl (males), or at least 55 mg/dl (females). Yes _____
10. In the midst of stressful situations (e.g., confrontations with students, parents, or others), I actually utilize, in at least 80 percent of such instances, appropriate breathing and large-muscle relaxation techniques to help myself feel more in control. Yes _____

How did you do?

There were 23 items in the list. If I were looking at your written responses (and non-responses) in each of the five sections, I'd be delighted if you were able to answer "yes" to:

- more than two (of six) in the "Degree of Isolation" section;
- more than one (of three) in the "Success Criteria" section;
- either (of two) in the "Long-term Professional Growth" section;
- either (of two) in the "Time for Analysis and Reflection" section;
- more than four (of 10) in the "Stress Patterns and Levels" section.

High-Energy Teaching: Improving the Odds

With this informal self-assessment fresh in your mind, let me give you a look, in advance, at the perspectives I take in *High-Energy Teaching* on the issues raised in each of these sections. I'd like you to see exactly what kinds of ideas I'll invite you to consider or reconsider throughout.

The following table, "Summary of Personal/Professional Issues," gives an overview-at-a-glance of what I'll urge you to do or not do.

Summary of Personal/Professional Issues

Category	Importance for renewal and psychological/emotional health	Accessibility: can be improved on your own without administrative/collegial assistance and support
Degree of Isolation	moderate	not accessible; difficult to improve without help
Success Criteria	moderate	not accessible; difficult to improve without help
Long-term Professional Growth	high	accessible; can be changed for the better on your own
Time for Analysis and Reflection	high	accessible; can be changed for the better on your own
Stress Patterns and Levels	high	accessible; can be changed for the better on your own

Degree of Isolation

Importance for Renewal and Personal/Professional Health: Moderate

Accessibility Without Administrative/Collegial Help: Not Accessible

Those six items, listed again:

1. I have a total of at least one hour's worth of *substantive*, solution-focused conversation with at least one colleague every week.
2. I team-teach or co-teach with at least one colleague, for at least one class session, at least once every week.
3. I have easy, comfortable access to at least one colleague for help with classroom problems, and actually use this access route regularly (at least twice a month).
4. I have reliable means for learning about my colleagues' successful and unsuccessful practices (access to a "technical/professional culture").
5. Faculty (or division or department) meetings are held at least weekly, and provide opportunities to discuss – in professional, problem-focused and problem-solving terms – *substantive* instructional issues at some length (more than 20 minutes, in each instance).
6. The faculty culture in my school is supportive – that is, I have plenty of evidence, readily and regularly apparent, that my colleagues value me for my efforts with our students.

Does it really matter whether or not you are professionally isolated? Do you feel you are doing well despite your isolation? Do you actually prefer isolation to interaction with your colleagues?

Without exception, organizational analyses of any kind of organization conclude that professional isolation, *while it may be convenient,* robs most professionals of a major source for intellectual stimulation; of a major source for new content, technique, and other ideas; of a major impetus for career planning and development; and of a major source for interpersonal "stress shaping."

However, you have seen from the summary chart that I consider your professional isolation to be of only "moderate" importance in your renewal and personal/professional health quest, and, further, to be unalterable without administrative and/or collegial assistance.

So, what do I think you should try to do about the degree of isolation you currently experience?

- If you are among the minority of teachers who are in a position to exercise real (formal or informal) leadership within your faculty, and if you have that bent, act upon the six items listed under this heading ("Degree of Isolation") within your own organization. Use your formal or informal organizational influence to lead your colleagues toward an altered faculty culture, faculty interaction system, and faculty support system. Establish these six items as goals, solicit support for them, and begin implementation (and, of course, evaluation) of them.
- If you are not in a position to exercise formal or informal leadership within your faculty (and I assume this is the case with the majority of readers), I urge you to accept your isolation – for the time being.

Here's why: You can "save yourself" by attacking along the lines I am about to recommend under the subsections titled "Long-term Professional Growth," "Time for Analysis and Reflection," and "Stress Patterns and Levels" – and these categories do not require administrative/collegial assistance for their implementation.

You have to save yourself, sometimes, before you can do anything else. As time passes, and as your personal/professional renewal program moves you quietly in the directions you set for yourself, others may notice.

They may ask for your help. If they do, you'll give it.

Eventually, you may actually find yourself with a cadre of colleagues – maybe just two or three others, or maybe most of your faculty – that is working with you in mutual support. At that point, whether you intended it or not, you will have become a leader within your faculty. And then, if you wish, you may reconsider organizational steps toward formal implementation of the six items listed at the start of this subsection.

Or you may not.

It may be true, by then, that six formal steps designed to correct the "degree of isolation" prevalent in your faculty will no longer seem very important. And in fact, by then, they may not be.

Success Criteria

Importance for Renewal and Personal/Professional Health: Moderate

Accessibility Without Administrative/Collegial Help: Not Accessible

Those three items, listed again:

1. I am provided with reliable data regarding my students' success or lack of success at the next levels of schooling (or in job settings, if that is the next step for some of them).
2. It is realistically possible for me to collect information on my own about individual students' success at the next levels of schooling (or in job settings, where appropriate).
3. I am able to assess *objectively and accurately* the progress that individual, and groups of, students make while under my tutelage each year (by means of, for example, pre- and post-tests systematically administered, or individualized software programs that electronically track student progress throughout the year).

Does it really matter whether or not you are in a position to realistically assess your own excellence by learning exactly how the "graduates" from your classes do at the next levels? Are you satisfied by knowing they seem to get promoted to further levels, or ultimately get into college or into the job market successfully? Is it good enough just to perceive progress as they pass through your hands?

Other kinds of organizations – other industries – have learned to go to enormous lengths to collect this kind of information, and then to alter their approaches as needed to enhance the quality of their work. But, as noted previously in this chapter, students' long-term success is so remote from your classroom, and so many other variables impinge upon their success, that this crucial information seems nearly impossible to gather in schools. In fact, even within-school-year progress is an elusive variable to harness.

You have seen from the summary chart that I consider a system for measuring success criteria to be of only "moderate" importance in your renewal and personal/professional health quest, and, further, to be out of reach without administrative and/or collegial assistance.

So, what do I think you should try to do about the paucity of available success criteria?

Only a little. These kinds of data are so problem-filled methodologically, I suggest you concentrate on collecting, especially in the fall, some anecdotal information: from individual teachers who teach your "graduates" immediately after they leave you, from some of the students' parents, and, if you're teaching older kids, from the students themselves (including college freshmen and those who have joined the work force or the military).

By structuring your questions just a little (for example, "How is Rosa doing this year with her long division?" rather than, "How is Rosa doing?"), you may actually get a better sense than you now have for whether or not you're accomplishing some of the specific goals you have for your students and yourself. And if you get a hint that you are not, in some particular area, you may be able to follow up more systematically in your anecdotal data-collection efforts, and then, of course, in your classroom approaches.

My main point here, though, is the same as my main point under the previous subheading. Both "Degree of Isolation" and "Success Criteria," for most teachers seeking efficient, workable ways to create a self-renewal program for themselves, should stay on those teachers' back burners for some time, and maybe permanently.

Most of the teachers with whom I have worked, and whom I have observed and spoken to in recent years, will find themselves more successful if they attack the next three subsections, and focus upon them as the core of their renewal/performance/health/stress programs: "Long-term Professional Growth," "Time for Analysis and Reflection," and "Stress Patterns and Levels."

Long-term Professional Growth

Importance for Renewal and Personal/Professional Health: High

Accessibility Without Administrative/Collegial Help: Accessible

Those two items, listed again:

1. My school (or system or district) encourages individual teachers to develop long-term professional growth plans, and then provides financial and other assistance in moving toward the planned goals. (This does not refer to graduate study or graduate degrees, though these could be included as elements in such a plan. This means, instead, planned movement toward intellectual, teaching-related fields of interest, toward teaching-technique skills acquisition, toward intellectual and/or skill-related "re-tooling" for predicted new frontiers in relevant teaching fields.)
2. In the absence of any school (or system or district) support, it is realistically possible for me to develop and implement my own long-term professional growth plan, as just described.

You have seen from the summary chart that I consider "Long-term Professional Growth" both "high" in importance for renewal and personal/professional health, and "accessible" to you with or without administrative/collegial assistance and support. But you have also read, in Dr. McLaughlin's comments, that her surveyed teachers "see no professional growth ahead and rarely experience a sense of personal or intellectual growth."

I think this comes mainly from the confusion inadvertently built into a salary system which, in most public schools and in many non-public schools, rewards teachers for: (1) years of teaching service; and (2) graduate credits and graduate degrees earned.

Nothing fuzzy there. That is a "clean" system. You look down the left column of a chart to find your years of teaching service, run your finger across the page to the column that shows your total graduate school credit and/or degree, and there it is! Your professional "value," expressed in dollars.

For your renewal and long-term professional growth, the problem is that nothing in all that graduate course work may be either of interest or of value to you. And this can turn the best of us into cynics.

Here you are, toiling away to earn graduate credits so you can "professionally develop," when, in fact, you may only be moving yourself one column to the right on the pay scale. This is a deadly combination to human beings who entered teaching for the "right" reasons.

Those reasons centered around a true sense of VOCATION – a sense of personal/professional mission and service to humankind, coupled with an assessment of yourself as someone who would flourish in that setting *and* make a real contribution.

That sense of mission and service actually runs counter to the materialistic, pragmatic, administrative, procedural, and enormously time-intensive process of attending graduate classes, semester after semester. This is not to say, you understand, that no graduate classes are of value. Some are magnificent, as are the professors teaching them. There is less chance, however, for even the strongest graduate classes to be meaningful, because crassly materialistic motivating factors so often play through the decision-to-enroll process.

Consequently, here is still another area related to your personal/professional self-renewal in which the odds are long against meaningful growth. Most of you will find that the "growth ideas" most closely related to your original, emotional impetus toward teaching have to do with one or more of the following: a particular content area (e.g., biology, math, literature), psychology (especially, the psychology of development and maturation), sociology (especially, the sociology of interpersonal relationships), or, especially, service (usually conceived in social, religious, and/or moral and philosophical terms).

Note that these are not grade-level specific. Teachers of second-graders may have received their first impetus from a fascination with foreign language; teachers of sophomores may have received their first impetus from the highly moral idea of service to young people and society.

Now, the bottom line.

If you were moved to teaching by one kind of factor (academic, emotional, moral, social, etc.), but your professional growth plan bears no relationship to that factor, you are most unlikely to find real professional growth – except, of course, on the salary chart. Worse, even the best of you may fall prey to the cynicism implicit in such a process.

I *am* a realist. You *do* need a good salary. Fine. If you need to move along on the salary scale, and if graduate courses move you along, then do not let me slow you down.

But – no matter what – make a Professional Development Plan for yourself that actually means something to you, that relates to self-renewal, and that stimulates you intellectually and emotionally. If you can fit that into your graduate work, good. If you can fit that into your continuing education units, good, too. But if you cannot, pursue both avenues: the credit path that leads to a livable salary and the renewal path that leads to a recovery of the "meaning."

That may mean you spend eight hours a week attending a graduate class, traveling to and from the class, and studying for that class, while you spend only 15 minutes a week on your "meaningful" professional growth activity.

Your "meaningful" professional growth activity may center on the writings of a particular author (who may or may not be writing about classrooms, but instead, about African history or business/organizational renewal or Russian society). Or your "meaningful" professional growth activity may be something you do: service in a homeless center, writing for publication or for fun, informal research in or out of your field, participation in a conference for the "right" reasons.

If you already engage in activities like that, then you know what I mean. But I still have a question. Have you placed all this into a long-term Professional Development Plan for yourself? Have you mapped out a general direction for yourself as an intellectual/emotional human being who – unless you are very different from the rest of us – needs a sense of direction, of anticipation, of purposeful movement in order to have a sense right now of ongoing renewal, of freshness, of gratification and self-worth?

This can be done. And creating your plan is not dependent on administrative/collegial support. It can be added to, or built around your graduate school commitment.

To know whether or not you already have what I mean, ask this. Am I really looking forward to what I expect to learn (in my professional growth plan) in the next 12 months? In the next three years? In the next decade?

The question is not: Do I have something written on paper? The question is: Am I excited?

Time for Analysis and Reflection

Importance for Renewal and Personal/Professional Health: High

Accessibility Without Administrative/Collegial Help: Accessible

Those two items, listed again:

1. For a total of at least 60 minutes a month, time is provided in my professional day for analysis of my teaching work, either aided by a colleague or alone. (This does not refer to "planning periods.")
2. For a total of at least 60 minutes a month, I create time for "Ritual Reflection" and recommitment to my vocation, and for reflection (in that context) on the quality and effectiveness of my teaching efforts.

I have written in the summary chart that "Time for Analysis and Reflection" is both of "high" importance for renewal and personal/professional health, and "accessible" without administrative/collegial support. You understand, then, that I consider this to be one of several keys to successful renewal.

Let me start by making clear that I do understand the problem.

My astonishment was palpable when, 20 years ago, I received my teaching schedule upon arrival at St. Lawrence University in upstate New York. My doctoral degree was fresh, but almost as fresh was my recollection of my teaching schedule in public schools.

My schedule in public schools looked like yours does now: a daily "planning period" in which I never planned, because I always needed to grade papers or meet with students or meet with parents or meet with somebody else at that time; at least one "duty time" each day in which I was required to supervise lunch lines or playgrounds or something; and at least 25 and usually 30 solid hours per week of scheduled teaching, face-to-face with students.

My St. Lawrence schedule struck me as a clerical error. Nine hours per week? (Actually less, because each of my three classes lasted two hours, 45 minutes, not three hours, and since each class had lengthy breaks, during which, of course, there was nothing to supervise.)

So, really, my responsibilities included about seven and one-half hours per week of teaching, no discipline problems, no lunch lines to supervise, no parent conferences, and no concession-stand duties at the basketball games.

Furthermore, since my three St. Lawrence University courses were all graduate courses for school teachers and administrators, two of them started at 4 p.m. and lasted until 6:45, while the other started at 7 p.m. and ended at 9:45. On no day was I scheduled to teach anything before late afternoon. For a person accustomed to being in full teaching harness by 8 a.m., five days a week, and arriving at school much earlier than that, most days, to prepare for classes, to supervise bus unloading or hallways, and to participate in hurried, 20-minute faculty meetings, this all seemed preposterous.

Of course, it wasn't long until my days were filled with research projects, university committee meetings, on-site "doings" with the area schools, and so on. But what never left me was a sense of absolute wonder at the amount of "time for analysis and reflection." It really mattered.

Any strong, central commitment which people make in their lives requires attention to renewal and recommitment. Good marriages attend to this. Good business organizations attend to this. Good religious organizations attend to this.

How is it, then, that so few of us as public or non-public school teachers build into our personal/professional lives a regular, "ritual" recommitment to our chosen vocation? Why is it that most of us seem to expect an ongoing sense of excitement and renewal without special effort on our parts?

There is time to do what I mean by this. I mean setting aside about an hour, on one day (not necessarily a school day) every month, to renew the "spirit of purpose" with which you and I launched this career. (When you rated yourself in the category of "Time for Analysis and Reflection," the second item read: "For a total of at least 60 minutes a month, I create time for 'Ritual Reflection' and recommitment to my vocation.")

This is not complicated. And there is no "correct" way to spend the 60 minutes (although I'm going to be pretty explicit in Chapter 9 about this).

As with any regular recommitment you might undertake, you could combine recollection (of your original purposes, of your own inspirational Prime Movers, of your own finest moments in teaching) with thoughtful self-assessment and re-examination of your own Professional Development Plan. And you could – and almost certainly should – conclude with a mental-emotional "fix" on the mind-set advocated throughout *High-Energy Teaching*: no renewal "from a distance." Immersion with the kids. Right now.

In Chapter 9, I will provide you with specific "attitude shapers," any of which can be plugged into the Ritual Reflection time that you set aside for yourself. I will also provide, in that chapter and in other chapters of the book, sample log sheets for you to use. Some of you will want to reflect upon previous reflections, and some of you will also want to track the progression of your renewal process over periods of time.

Stress Patterns and Levels

Importance for Renewal and Personal/Professional Health: High

Accessibility Without Administrative/Collegial Help: Accessible

Those 10 items, listed again:

1. On an average of three days per week or more, year-round, I feel invigorated and fulfilled at the end of the school day.
2. For well over half the total weeks in the school year, I find myself looking forward on Sunday evening to Monday morning at school.
3. Most of the time (four hours or more), on most days (three per week or more), throughout the school year, I find myself "lost in my work" – in the best sense of that phrase – enjoying the give-and-take of the teaching/learning experience, gratified by a "background" sense of doing meaningful service, and actually happy to be where I am.
4. Most of the time (at least 15 out of every 20 working days, year-round) I am absolutely without stress symptoms (e.g., stomach problems, headaches, a heightened sense of anxiety, a feeling of malaise, mild depression, persistent fatigue).
5. Most of the time (at least 15 out of every 20 working days, year-round) I am "even-tempered" in my classroom. (This implies that confrontations with students are reasoned, on the teacher's part, and not self-destructive to the teacher emotionally, psychologically, or physically; this does not imply a low frequency of confrontations.)
6. As an indicator of my overall health and ability to perform daily tasks, I know what my diastolic and systolic blood pressure readings are on a weekly basis, year-round.

7. My diastolic blood pressure never exceeds 85.
8. I know what my HDL and LDL cholesterol readings are, at my peak stress period(s) per school-year cycle (late spring for many teachers, according to the CTR pilot study).
9. My HDL cholesterol reading, at my peak stress period(s), is at least 43 mg/dl (males), or at least 55 mg/dl (females).
10. In the midst of stressful situations (e.g., confrontations with students, parents, or others), I actually utilize, in at least 80 percent of such instances, appropriate breathing and large-muscle relaxation techniques to help myself feel more in control.

Notice how careful I am not to use the terms "stress management" or "stress control." Neither term tells people what I mean. That's why I prefer the phrase "stress shaping."

"Stress management" seems to mean, to most people, relaxing. People usually picture techniques such as meditation, progressive relaxation, or massage. But those have nothing to do with what I mean.

"Stress control" seems to mean, to most people, manipulation of environmental factors and/or internal (mental-physical) factors to hit just the right stress level for a given circumstance. This is closer to what I mean. But the word "control" implies too much.

"Stress shaping" says the right thing. It says that you and I can influence our own responses to environmental factors and to internal factors, and that we can be very proactive about it.

Exactly.

We can be proactive about it, and, as classroom teachers, we'd better be. You see, your body's own stress response can lower your ability to fight diseases and it can lower your ability to respond effectively when you're in the middle of a stressful situation. I'll explain more about your body's response to stress in Chapter 7. And I'll present you with a series of stress shapers from which you can pick and choose.

These are approaches, techniques, and lifestyle elements, which through years of research, counseling, and classroom work, I have found to be most likely actually to be put to use by people who rarely can take "time out" to relax. Please understand that I do not expect you to attempt them all. Certainly, if you did, and if you tried to master them all, you could be overwhelmed.

So, keep this perspective in mind. To become nicely "stress-shaped," you'll only need to get really good at a few of these approaches, techniques, and lifestyle elements.

Granted, any of them will take self-discipline and determination on your part. Sometimes people will say, "Can you just take 15 minutes or so and give me the highlights of stress shaping, so I can get through this week (or month, or semester, or year)?" Well ... no. Every single piece of this requires much more than that.

You can do this. I'll give you only the approaches that people have liked, and have been willing to use. But you'll have to get serious about it. We're talking about your *life* here.

Section II:

Teaching Is Leadership
Teaching Is Knowledge
Teaching Is Relationships

Chapter 4

Off-center Leadership

What image enters your mind when you picture a teacher who is a "good leader" in the classroom? And what words or phrases accompany that image?

Do these fit?

- Charismatic
- Dynamic
- Forceful
- Energetic
- Decisive
- Powerful
- Articulate
- Compelling

In most people's minds, they do seem to fit.

But I think that most of those words miss the mark. "Energetic" is okay. But the others – "charismatic, dynamic, forceful, decisive, powerful, articulate, compelling" – just do not seem to me to get at the heart of what defines leadership *in the eyes of the followers – the kids themselves – in classrooms.*

I think the following words constitute the "right" list.

- Confrontational
- Respectful
- Persistent
- Unconventional
- Unself-conscious
- Morally courageous

Guy Doud, a former national Teacher of the Year, whose experiences as a sixth-grade student I will describe in Chapter 9, strikes me as a superior teacher/leader. But when I watch him on a 60-minute video tape, I'm struck by how little his personal style fits the stereotypical "leader." He's not afraid to laugh at his own foibles, to poke fun at his former state of obesity, or to sing a hokey farewell song to students graduating from his class. He comes across, frankly, as a little off-center. And I mean that as high praise.

It seems obvious to me that he isn't concerned, really, about what we think of him. He *is* concerned about his teaching message and his teaching mission, and about what you and I – his "learners" – are learning and experiencing. He's *pushy*, in fact, about those things, in a friendly, respectful sort of way. And that, I'm convinced, is what leadership really means for classroom teachers. Not charismatic, dynamic, forceful, and the other typical "leadership" images. Instead, confrontational-yet-respectful, persistent, unself-conscious, morally courageous.

This has importance beyond what you may at first imagine. In the CTR's ongoing research project, we find that students perform consistently well (in terms of their grades) in classrooms in which the teachers operate in certain ways.[1] The theme of those "certain ways" is embodied in Dr. Martin E. P. Seligman's concepts of "learned helplessness" and "learned optimism."[2]

---

1 See my 1992 book, *Twenty Principles for Teaching Excellence,* and Appendix, pages 175-181.

2 For more on the ideas that undergird these formulations, see Seligman's outstanding volume, *Learned Optimism*, New York: Knopf, 1991, and *Psychopathology: Experimental Models*, San Francisco: Freeman, 1977.

In simplest terms: Each time you, through your actions or words, reinforce your students positively or negatively for something they've said or done, you strengthen the connection in their brains between their efforts to do something and the results of their efforts.

To quote from *Teaching Excellence*:

> When humans see no connection between what they try to do and the apparent result, their mind-sets move toward a "learned helpless" condition. Conversely, when humans do see a clear connection between what they try to do and the apparent result, their mind-sets move toward the "learned optimistic" condition. Learned helplessness is associated with lack of persistence and (in the CTR study) with deterioration in performance. Learned optimism is associated with determination, resilience, and (in the CTR study) with consistent, high-level performance. Both mind-sets are learnable – and teachable.
>
> Think about the last time – yesterday, maybe – you went home from school feeling vaguely down, a little depressed, somewhat discouraged, lacking enthusiasm. Why was that? Seligman's ideas, as applied here, would imply that even though you worked hard to teach your students throughout the day, *you saw no obvious connections between what you tried to do and the apparent result.* No big problems occurred; no huge failures or blow-ups transpired. But the connections you needed to see between your efforts and your efforts' results were inconspicuous to you.
>
> Ask yourself this. How many consecutive days would that need to happen before your performance began to be affected? Two? Five? Ten? Twenty? Fifty? A semester's worth?

The implication of all this is that none of us can maintain high-energy teaching without *great* attention to continuous positive and negative reinforcement of our students. And that means "immersion" with them. Continual interaction. Energy. Vigor. Persistence on our parts.

In earlier chapters of this book, I insisted: "No renewal from a distance." Exactly. And at this point I am insisting: "No consistently high-level student performance from a distance, either."

Your own renewal requires immersion with the kids. Not coincidentally, *getting consistently high-level performance from them requires the same thing.*

Guts

What just happened?

I think that I redefined "Leadership." Didn't I?

I think I made a case for the idea that leadership in classrooms has to do with your willingness to immerse yourself with the students, in a certain spirit-of-interaction. Confrontational-yet-respectful. Persistent. Unself-conscious. Morally courageous. A sort of SUPPORTIVE HOUNDING, if you will. Having the guts to be, in the Guy Doud manner, a little off-center in the persistence of your interaction with them, your unwillingness to let them drift along, your determination to let them know where you stand and what you think of their efforts.

This is leadership in classrooms. It's the only kind that matters.

So, what if you are *also* charismatic, dynamic, forceful, and all the other, more conventional leader-ly things? Is that good or not?

Well, surely it's good.

It's just not what makes the difference.

It's the *other* list that makes the difference – both in how well the kids respond academically (and in lots of other ways), *and* in whether or not you're likely to experience renewal of the kind I mean in this book.

How High the Risk?

But this course can be perilous.

If you distance yourself from the students – teaching-from-a-distance – you can conserve your emotional and physical energy. Because you'll have (by definition) less feedback from them, and less two-way reinforcement, you can tell yourself every day that you did fine, and that things went well, and that the kids probably learned stuff.

And then you may find that you'll fit right in with Milbrey McLaughlin's Rand Corporation survey (Chapter 2). You'll be in the majority. You'll be among those serving out their time as educators. Working conscientiously, certainly. But without excitement, spirit, exalted hopes, and the consuming, high-energy enthusiasm for this career that is essential for your own renewal and for the students' performance. The whole depressing, but safe, career-teaching scenario.

Is the other worth the risk? I don't know.

Immersion of the kind I mean entails the loss of any illusions you might have had about just how well your students are doing, and about what they really care about (or could be *led through a certain kind of off-center leadership to care about*), and about what they really think of you (or could be *led* to think of you).

It will mean that you go home every single day having been more strongly reinforced than ever before on the continuum of your own learned helplessness and learned optimism. You'll be so immersed every day with the students that you'll multiply the number of times you find, or do not find, self-perceived connections between your efforts, and the outcomes of your efforts.

Okay.

And what if you do immerse yourself, and depart from the safety of teaching-from-a-distance, and find every day that you've moved further and further in the direction of learned helplessness, not of learned optimism? What if you find that every day you teach, you perceive an insufficient relationship between what you're trying so hard to do and the results – in your students' responses – of what you're trying to do? What then?

Well, that's the risk. How much of a "leadership risk" are you willing to take to achieve both the consistently high-level student performance I talk about, and the renewal of your spirit of commitment that I also talk about?

Heroism

I recently read a newspaper article about a first-year teacher, a recent college graduate, working with inner-city third-graders. I studied the reporter's narrative coverage of this young woman's first four months of teaching. I saw how frequently she despaired of making any difference in the lives of her young charges. I saw how quickly – even in her first day in the classroom – she moved toward the learned-helplessness end of the continuum, how immediately she sensed "no connection" between her efforts and the outcomes of her efforts.

But I also saw her young energy at work. I saw her persistence. I saw her immense, quiet, moral courage, her insistence on letting her kids know where she stood, even when she hadn't the remotest idea what she "ought" to be working toward with them.

And I was struck by the reporter's moving account of this teacher's return to school on the Monday after Thanksgiving break. The reporter described how the teacher climbed the steps to her classroom, apprehensive. As the classroom door came into her line of vision, the face of one of her young students happened to be turned toward the hallway. The child's face instantly brightened, and the teacher was able to read her student's lips as she reported happily to a classmate *"Ms. ______________ is here!"*

That moment spoke volumes to this struggling teacher. And it meant everything to her, *for a while*. That child had unwittingly moved her teacher an enormous distance on the learned helplessness/learned optimism continuum, away from the learned-helplessness end near which she hovered so much of the time. Suddenly, this teacher could say to herself: "Yes! I do matter!" And, had she been acquainted with these learned helplessness/learned optimism ideas, she might have added: "My persistence is not without reward. There *is* a connection between my efforts and the results of my efforts."

Will it be enough? From a research standpoint, I can say that persistence in any endeavor is a function of whether or not you can be effective enough, in your own eyes, to move yourself toward the learned optimism end of this continuum. Effective *in your own eyes* at a level that keeps you motivated to continue in those efforts.

If you cannot maintain this sense of "relatedness" (of your own efforts to your perceived outcomes), you may still choose to continue, whether your endeavor consists of being a student, a teacher, a spouse, a parent, or something else. *But it is likely to be in a spirit of resignation and perhaps of desperation – and possibly, as well, of cynicism.*

And so we find around us the resigned, the desperate, the cynical:

students, teachers, parents, and spouses, continuing in the endeavor, but without expectation and without a sense of meaning.

My wish for that first-year teacher is that she continue to display the "magnificent" (a carefully chosen word here) *leadership* she has displayed to this point in her fledgling career. My wish is that she experience many more bits and pieces of evidence that demonstrate that her efforts are causing results. My wish is that these pieces of evidence come increasingly frequently to her – which is a very real possibility, given the extent of her immersion and her determination to become technically better as a professional – so that she may develop a pervasive sense of learned optimism about herself as a classroom leader.

And my wish, finally, is this: If she cannot "win" this internal battle for the high ground of learned optimism, I hope she either shifts permanently to a different career, or that she leaves this profession for several years to gain psychological, physical, and emotional maturity in preparation for re-entry. Above all, my wish is that she not give up her leadership style for the alternative: teaching-from-a-distance, the lethal retreat from immersion to the safety of a self-deluding mediocrity-of-commitment.

Whatever becomes of this young woman, in her first semester of teaching she illustrates exactly the brand of heroism that ultimately – if maintained – will make her the Prime Mover for literally hundreds of youthful human beings whose lives she will move in undreamed of directions.

Chapter 5

The Complicated and the Merely Difficult

Not long ago I had the luxury of visiting a school just for fun. My agenda called only for observing and learning – not "researching," consulting, or recommending. Although the school's novel approach to the use of computer instruction in K-5 served as the attraction, I spent time in a dozen or more classrooms at all levels, just getting a sense of the place.[1] Three teachers, in particular, got my attention during that day.

I can picture the science instructor for the junior high students. For one class period, I sat with the kids as he taught a combination of physics, chemistry, and electronics to about 25 seventh-graders. This teacher was a very young man. I'm not certain, after just one class period of observation, whether his leadership approach would qualify as "off-center." But I think so.

What gripped me most in that short time was the breadth of his knowledge. And that, it seemed to me, is also what gripped the students so powerfully. This class period marked a *tour de force* the likes of which I had not seen for a while.

His level of learned optimism must have been extremely high, because not only were the kids rapt in their attentiveness to his several mini-lectures (five to 10 minutes each) during the period, but he led them, in addition, through several demonstrations, using materials at their tables. In so doing, he "proved" his lectures, immersed himself and

---

1 The Waterford School is a non-public (independent) school in Sandy, Utah.

the kids in the process, and, via the proving and the immersing and the demonstrating and the kid-responding, he provided himself with unmistakable evidence that *there were connections between his efforts and the outcomes of his efforts.*

Later that day, I spent half an hour with a second-grade teacher whose students were working on language skills. While I understood less of this process than I had of the seventh-graders' science class, I was again struck by how much this young woman *knew* about the "languaging" process, and about how kids do and do not become more proficient with it.

And then there was the senior English seminar. On that particular February day, the seniors themselves did most of the presenting. But once more I was fascinated by how much the teacher knew about the variety of topics under examination. Occasionally, he said, "I don't know." More often, he could supply the complementary idea that transformed a fragmented presentation into a credible construct.

Based on those three cursory classroom visits, I couldn't guess the extent to which those three teachers were experiencing a sense of renewal, of career excitement, or of learned optimism. I can only say that their academic grasp of subject matter, their apparent pleasure in their knowledge, and the extent to which their knowledge bases were current helped give them force as teachers, well beyond that which I often observe in classrooms. Their command of material seemed to envelop their students at least as much as it did me.

Let me ask the question: How current is your knowledge base right now?

A Prominent Irony

One of the ironic characteristics of teaching is how very easy it is to stagnate intellectually. Does any profession even approach ours on that score? If you will think back to Chapter 2 ("Long Odds and the Big Picture"), you may incline, as I do, toward a "No." McLaughlin's list was depressing: teachers' isolation from their colleagues; the astonishing absence of a common *technical/professional culture*; the near impossibility of accurately self-assessing their long-term impact; the depressing finding from the survey that teachers see before them no opportunities for personal, *intellectual* or professional growth.

Each of those phrases would raise a red flag for most professionals in other fields. "What," they would ask, "is going on here?"

Dr. Stephen Covey, in his hugely successful book, *Principle-Centered Leadership*[2] (a sequel to his equally successful *The Seven Habits of Highly Effective People*), makes a forceful case for linkage among four leadership factors: competence, character, trustworthiness, and ongoing professional development.

Covey writes that coworkers trust you based on what you are as a person – your character – and what you can do – your competence. Professionals can lose their trustworthiness when they allow themselves to become obsolete within the work place, when they fail to maintain both character and competence. Maintaining – and improving – character and competence is achieved through purposeful, ongoing professional development.

Regardless of whether or not you have a Professional Development Plan in writing (or in your head), my question remains: "Are you *excited* about what your plan implies?" Are you actually looking forward to what you expect to learn as part of your plan, not only in the short-term, but over the long haul of your career? From where you stand, is one of the major benefits of teaching the fact that you have the opportunity continually to learn more about the things which *intellectually* you find most stimulating? Are you, in short, frequently in the mode of learner, and do you have a plan to remain in that mode?

I consider Long-term Professional Growth a personal/professional process of high importance for your renewal and psychological/emotional health, and something you can plan and implement on your own.

How would I suggest you do it? Please examine the chart on the pages following this one.

---

2 Covey, Stephen R., *Principle-Centered Leadership*, New York: Simon & Schuster, 1992.

Your Professional Development Plan: A Framework

In order to develop your own Professional Development Plan, think back to this book's earlier chapters, and accept or reject each of the following four assumptions. Keep your acceptance or rejection of the four assumptions in mind as you proceed through the framework following.

Four Assumptions

1. The "most renewing" Professional Development Plan for me will help re-connect me to my First Purposes (my original rational/emotional impetus for pursuing a teaching career). Yes____ No____
2. My Professional Development Plan has as one of its primary purposes the rekindling of my personal/professional enthusiasm and commitment to my profession. Yes____ No____
3. My Professional Development Plan has as its other primary purpose the stimulation of my *intellectual* interests, as those interests relate to my teaching career. Yes____ No____
4. My Professional Development Plan can be designed by me and implemented by me completely without – if necessary – the assistance and cooperation of my colleagues and my administration. Yes____ No____

A Framework

With your responses to the four assumptions in mind, work within the following framework to develop an outline for your Professional Development Plan. If you rejected one, two, three, or all four of the assumptions, be careful to modify the framework as appropriate, so that your completed outline is consistent with your assumptions.

1. List the elements in your academic roots. (Ask: "What individual teachers were involved in my earliest excitement about the subject matter and/or classroom processes in which I am currently involved?" And: "What, specifically, in their presentations of subject matter and/or process, first got my attention, led me to think about their material outside of class, and, ultimately, may have been involved in my decision to undertake a career in teaching?")

*Teachers' or professors' names*____

____

____

Subject(s) (e.g., reading, childhood development, biology, literature)

____

____

____

*Memorable academic events*____

____

____

____

____

____

____

*My responses to those events (my hopes, expectations)*____________________

____

____

____

____

____

____

2. Record on the next page the extended details of your responses, hopes, and expectations, as those relate to your early experiences. (Ask: "What plans – whether related explicitly to teaching or not – began to form in my mind? What actions did I ultimately take? What course did I set out to follow?")

*Early plans*____

*Early actions*____

*Early course followed*__________________________________

3. Record the barriers you have encountered in the process of "working your plan." (Ask: "What has stood in the way of the accomplishment of my original plans/actions/course?") Your barriers may have included family commitments, lack of money, procrastination, a gradual fading of your commitment, a loss of the "spirit of commitment" (coupled, maybe, with disillusionment or even cynicism), the loss of a personal/professional vision of the future, or a conscious rejection of your First Purposes.

*Barriers*____

4. Record below the mid-course corrections you have implemented in response to "real life conditions" encountered along the way. (Ask: "What professional development steps – graduate courses, workshops, in-service programs, personal/professional reading programs – have I actually undertaken as the months and years have passed since my original commitment? How closely related were they to my original commitment? What, exactly, was the relationship of those professional development activities to my First Purposes?")

*Professional development steps (with approximate dates)*________________

Relationship of those steps to my First Purposes. (Rate each step on a 1-9 scale, with "9" indicating a step with the most powerful possible relationship to your First Purposes, and with "1" indicating a step that was utterly irrelevant to your First Purposes.)

5. Record below your assessment of the relationship of your professional development activities to your personal/professional renewal. (Ask: "Have my professional development activities contributed to my renewal process? In what ways?")

My professional development activities' relationship to my renewal process

6. Record below the impact of your professional development activities on the stimulation of your *intellectual* interests. (Ask: "Have my professional development activities excited me, intrigued me, and led me to think, *after* an activity's conclusion, about the ideas and concepts presented to me? Have I looked forward with an intellectual impatience to my next encounter with the activity? Were these activities comparable, as intellectually exciting events, to those which I have associated with my Prime Movers?")

Impact of my professional development activities on the stimulation of my intellectual interests. (List activities with approximate dates, together with your comments on the intellectual stimulation value of each.)

7. Think 10 years into the future. How would you like to picture yourself as a professional person? Do NOT in this exercise attempt to picture yourself in a completely different context. For this renewal-focused exercise to be valuable to you, imagine yourself in your current teaching context. *How would you have to "be," and what would you need to have learned, to find yourself an intellectually stimulated, emotionally fulfilled professional?* MAKE YOURSELF ANSWER THIS QUESTION. (If you want to imagine yourself in a different professional context, that's fine, but not in this exercise. Indulging in that fantasy, even if you are able to make it come true, will make every day in your current teaching context an exercise in unhappiness as you invest your emotional energy in wishing you were somewhere else.)

An ideal professional "me," 10 years from now. (List your needed personal/professional characteristics, and/or the concepts and skills you would need to have learned, in order to be fulfilled in *this* teaching context.)

____

____

____

____

____

____

____

____

____

____

____

Now write an outline for your Professional Development Plan by listing, on the next page, the major steps you could realistically take in the next month, the next six months, the next 12 months, the next two years, the next five years, the next 10 years and beyond, to move yourself toward the personal/professional characteristics you listed in #7.

If you accepted the four assumptions at the start of this exercise, your outline will help you to connect your Professional Development

Plan to your First Purposes, and/or rekindle your personal/professional enthusiasm and commitment to the profession, and/or spark a high level of stimulation of your intellectual interests. Avoid steps that require support or approval from other people, such as your colleagues or your family.

Reminder: *You can find "First-Purpose connectors," "rekindlers," and "intellectual stimulators" if you search explicitly for those*, rather than for "credit" (career ladder credit, graduate credit, continuing education credit, etc.) as your primary criterion. You *may* find both. Or you *may* have to choose between the two. Or you *may* successfully create parallel tracks for the two.

Examples include: commitment to your own Ritual Reflection program (see Chapter 9), *selective* enrollment in university course work (possibly as an auditor rather than as a for-credit student), the aggressive ferreting out of exciting workshops in your own academic and geographic areas, an informal "peer coaching" or "peer renewal" arrangement with a like-minded friend (see Chapter 12), or the formation of a "brown bag breakfast" group for monthly discussions on professionally stimulating topics.

An Outline for a Professional Development Plan

List major Professional Development Plan steps designed to move you toward the personal/professional characteristics you listed in #7. (Include, as appropriate, potential "First-Purpose connectors," "rekindlers," and "intellectual stimulators." Ask: "What do I need to learn? How would I proceed to learn it? How would I have to learn to 'be'?")

*Next 30 days*____

____

____

____

____

____

Next six months (include items from previous list, as needed)

Next 12 months (include items from previous lists, as needed)

Next two years (include items from previous lists, as needed)

Next five years (include items from previous lists, as needed)

Next 10 years and beyond (include items from previous lists, as needed)

The base questions, then, are these.

- What are my assumptions about my own ongoing renewal – about my own long-term professional development?
- Given those assumptions, what do I need to learn, in order to experience continual renewal and intellectual stimulation in this teaching context? Given those required, necessary, ongoing "learnings," how can I organize and plan my career in order to acquire them?

- And, finally, is capturing a "permanent" sense of excitement, stimulation, and career fulfillment important enough to justify overcoming the obstacles?

This really is not complicated. It is merely difficult. And the teachers I have known are not easily defeated.

Chapter 6

In With the Alligators

We were sure wrong about one thing.

When we started what we now call the CTR International Model Schools Project in 1989, we thought – and we were right about this – that student performance and stress would influence each other. But we thought the things that would "fix" the problems were mostly administrative: the school calendar, the daily schedule, the ways in which everything in the school was organized (or not organized).

We were wrong. Some of those things do matter, to a lesser or greater degree.[1] But what matters most is something very different. *What matters most is something we learned to call the "sense of community" experienced by the students, the faculty, and the administration.* Performance tends to be most consistent and to remain at highest levels when there is a strong sense that WE ARE ALL IN THIS TOGETHER. And the all-in-this-together feeling is mostly something that is engendered (or not) in a school's classrooms, one classroom at a time, one teacher at a time.

As a teacher, your standards can be as high as you want them to be, *provided* you are able to communicate to the kids that you are on their side, that you want their success, and that you strongly hope they can manage, with your help, to succeed. And if you really do hope that they'll succeed, you'll probably behave in certain teacher-ly ways that go hand-in-hand with that. Here are some of those ways:

---

1 These ideas were covered briefly in Chapter 2, and are described more fully in the Appendix.

- explicit and frequent statements of your expectations for the students;
- repeated articulation of your "vision" for them, of what you hope they'll achieve and become while they are with you, and after they leave you;
- careful development of your courses, units, and themes, *consistent with your stated expectations*;
- thoughtful preparation of your students for each of your "testing events" (anything that you evaluate) which, above all, must be seen as *fair* – in the students' eyes – and representative of what you've promised them you want them to learn, to understand, and to become.

Tricking the students on tests, then, is OUT. Using your tests as "teaching vehicles" is IN.

Using your tests as bludgeons to defeat as many of your students as possible is OUT. Using your tests as barometers allowing you to see whether or not you're really teaching them anything is IN.

Setting yourself up as the barrier the students must scale is OUT. Setting yourself up simultaneously as barrier *and* springboard over the barrier is IN.

Priding yourself on the high number of kids who can't make it in your class is OUT. Priding yourself on giving all your kids good marks in the mistaken belief that this builds self-esteem is ALSO OUT. Priding yourself on getting every kid up to a level at which she or he is *earning* a decent mark is IN.

Accepting a knowledge base for yourself (of both content and process) that just gets you by is OUT. Building your knowledge base to an extremely high level *so that you can be infinitely flexible during each lesson* is IN.

Letting students know (with a letter grade, only) at the end of each grading period whether they've done things well or poorly is OUT. Giving near-continuous positive and/or negative reinforcement, every time you see every student, is IN.

Teaching "from a distance" is OUT. "Immersion" with the students – in class, in the hallways, outside of school – is IN.

"Tears in His Eyes"

When the students perceive that you are "on their side" they'll feel that WE'RE ALL IN THIS TOGETHER. This is when they'll feel that a sense of community exists. This is also when *you'll* feel that a sense of community exists. This is when they'll see connections between their efforts and the outcomes of their efforts. And this is when they'll persist in their efforts, over time, and ultimately achieve consistent, high-level performance *because of how you are choosing to be with them.*

"High-level" is, of course, a relative term; it refers to a student's performing well, within her or his capacity. It does not refer to "giving" a student unearned good marks. And it does not refer to miracles, either, although those tend to come with remarkable frequency when this kind of "supportive hounding" emanates consistently from the teacher.

I wish you could sit in on some of our interviews with the students in the CTR project. Our staff members go on campus four times a year. We feared, early on, that there might be a connection between how well or poorly a particular student was doing with a particular teacher, on the one hand, and how that student would judge that particular teacher, on the other (as is the case in some studies with university-level student evaluations of professors).

But, possibly because the set of questions we ask are not very similar to those university-level evaluation instruments, that's not what we find. We find, instead, that a school's sense of community determines how kids talk about their teachers.

In School A, for example, with a strong sense of community, we may find that even the most academically marginal student will speak this way of her teacher(s): "Oh, yes, Mr. Jones gives me exactly the grades I earn (which, we interviewers know, are mostly D's and F's). He's very fair. It hurts him every time I don't have my work. Yesterday he had tears in his eyes when he realized I still didn't have my science report ready."

In School B, conversely, with little sense of community, we may find that even the academically superior student will speak of her teacher(s) with cold contempt: "No. I'm not graded fairly. If Mr. Smith can possibly trick us on his tests, he will. I get my A's because I won't let him beat me."

Now, if just one or two students in a given school speak that way about their teachers, it doesn't mean much in our study. But we tend to find consistency in the way students view their teachers, school to school.

That's why we talk about a "faculty culture."

What's yours like? Is it OK to be upbeat about the kids when you talk with your colleagues? Is it OK to talk about how excited you are about how some of the kids are doing? Is it OK to talk excitedly about what *you're* learning?

Or do your colleagues look at you funny if you speak that way about your profession? Is it OK to run the students down *ad infinitum*? Is it, instead, OK to criticize your colleagues (behind their backs, of course) – perhaps explicitly *because* one or several of them are trying new things, pursuing new ideas, "immersing" themselves with the kids, advancing their intellectual grasp of their material and/or their teaching/learning process, renewing themselves and their careers? Is it OK to criticize your administration, the parents of the kids, the district office or the trustees, the state-level administration, the national-level administration, etc.?

What is your faculty culture like? And if the negative elements just mentioned describe yours, what should you do about it?

I say start with your own renewal program, as I describe throughout this book. Engage one or two like-minded friends, either at your school or at some other, and begin a little support group. Immerse yourself with the kids, and receive your reinforcement – your "learned optimism" – from their responses to that immersion process. Display the "off-center leadership" characteristics that I described in Chapter 4. Go ahead and make a difference in the lives of these kids. This year.

Classroom Discipline

Have you heard Notre Dame coach Lou Holtz's alligator story?

It seems a wealthy rancher wanted to show off his new Olympic-sized swimming pool, so he invited the town folk out for a late afternoon poolside reception. But he didn't want any of them in the pool, so he laced it with alligators.

In mid-reception, made somewhat incoherent by his own libations, the rancher addressed the crowd: "I don't see enough examples of courage these days. I'd like to think our country is still filled with people of courage, but I just don't see much of it.

"So, I've decided to offer one of three prizes to the person among you who will dive into my Olympic-sized pool, fight through the alligators, and climb out of the pool on the other side. The prizes are: my daughter's hand in marriage, $5 million in cash, or the deed to my ranch.

"Will one of you accept my challenge? Does one of you have the courage to overcome these ferocious reptiles? Is there hope for the future of our country?"

He paused tipsily. No one stirred.

The rancher's head dropped to his chest, and he turned miserably to walk back into his palatial home.

No sooner had he turned his back than he heard a shout and a splash. For 22 minutes a young man fought his way through the snapping jaws of the alligators, emerging at length on the other side, scathed but alive.

The crowd cheered while the rancher rushed around the outside of the pool to the young man's side. Deliriously happy, the rancher babbled: "I had given up hope in America. You have restored my faith in our national courage.

"I am a man of my word. What is your wish: my daughter's hand in marriage, $5 million in cash, or the deed to my ranch?"

Exhausted, the young man fixed his eyes first upon the crowd on the other side of the pool, then on the rancher. "My wish," he said slowly, "is to know which one of those so-and-so's over there pushed me into that pool."

Yes, exactly. What some call "classroom discipline" or "class control" is the Olympic-sized alligator pool for teachers. None of us entered the profession because we dreamed of controlling unruly students. We got into the profession to teach. But that placed us in proximity to the alligator pool. And somebody pushed us in.

Why would 25 alligators – students – want to cooperate with you when you're trying to teach them something? Well, they might not. You *can* do certain things to increase your chances, though, of getting their cooperation.

As the experienced teachers among this book's readers have long since learned, you successfully "control your class" through a combination of factors. The following list includes the factors most compatible with establishing and maintaining a strong sense of community within your classroom.

- A superior grasp of your academic subject matter, regardless of your teaching level. Real *mastery* of developmental reading theory, or European history, or the earth sciences allows you to be infinitely flexible in your approach. It allows you even to have in your repertoire the "mid-period switch" in which you say to yourself, "This isn't working. I need to come at this from a different angle." And so you do.
- A willingness (and sufficient "energy") to overprepare. If you don't have a LOT for your class to do, and if you cannot create an aura of both relevance and importance around that "lot," the students – of any age – sense in a matter of seconds that none of this is very important. That being the case, why should these alligators do anything other than act like the reptiles they have the capacity to be?
- A willingness to engage in confrontation. And practice in doing it. My use of this term does not necessarily imply hostility. It implies exactly what the CTR project emphasizes: the essential nature of near-continuous reinforcement, both positive and negative. Near-continuous engagement with your students enables you to exchange the kind of information that allows you to know *there are connections between your efforts and the outcomes of your efforts*. Thus, from this, you get learned optimism, persistence, and consistent performance.

- In-action stress-shaping skills (coming, in Chapter 10). In students' eyes, your in-action stress-shaping skills translate into assertion. Those skills help you feel in control over your own responses to a stressful situation. You do not appear afraid. You appear to be doing your duty, without hesitation. You "present" to them, as a dispassionate reinforcer, the behaviors implied by the sense of community you seek to create. There is a "presence" about you.
- A consciousness of the probability that thorn-in-your-side students are almost certainly not out to "get" you, unless you give them real reason to – such as humiliating and demeaning them in the eyes of their peers. In fact, they are probably not even *thinking* about you. They are thinking about impressing their peers in general, about impressing a particular peer with whom they are falling in love, or about some wretched academic, social, or familial event that transpired within the last 24 hours. Thus, there is a very practical URGENCY in being considerate to your "thorns," even in the midst of confronting them about negative behavior. Confronting negative behavior, while remaining respectful of the person, goes a long way toward establishing the sense of community you want in your classroom.
- Instantaneous forgiveness, demonstrated through immediate involvement of student offenders in the community-building process: "Jane, Robert, Charles (the student confronted 60 seconds previously), Scott – please distribute these papers for me?"
- A year-long teaching plan for the development of your class control process. You do not expect your students to know much about your subject matter (content) in September; do not expect them to know much about how to *conduct* themselves in September, either. Plan to teach them, and to teach them continuously, throughout the year, just as with content.

If you never teach your behavior expectations effectively and early, expect to spend large amounts of time throughout the school year reteaching unlearned community-enhancing behaviors.

So, if you do all of that, and do it well, you'll have smooth sailing, right?

Not on your life.

But if you roll all the items in the just-completed list into a manageable whole, and persist in those approaches, you'll probably find yourself an "off-center leader."

I insisted in Chapter 4 that the sort of leadership consistent with sense of community, with high-level student performance, and with high-energy teaching was "off-center leadership," characterized more by "supportive hounding" than by the usual leadership markers. You can approach classroom discipline from either end: by thinking about off-center leadership, or by thinking about swimming through the alligator pool in the ways I just listed.

But the only way to have really smooth sailing is to star in your own movie. A television critic once noted that in "teacher movies," the star teacher always has just one group of kids. The star sees them once a day, and is free the rest of the time to save the students' lives in any number of ways.

Real-life, high-energy teaching doesn't provide a storybook existence, free of difficulties. *But it does give meaning and perspective to those difficulties*. And there, in that meaning and in that perspective, lies personal/professional renewal.

Section III:
Inner Workings: Stress Shaping

Chapter 7

Psychophysiology 101: Teaching From the Inside Out

Picture this.

You're taking an undergraduate course in "stress shaping" (but with some pretentious title like "The Psychophysiology of Stress"). It's time for the performance component of your final examination. You go to the instructor's office, enter, sit down in a cushioned chair, and watch him attach you to several biofeedback machines. Each machine, you're told, will be measuring a different aspect of your stress response (exactly like the notorious polygraph machine used as a lie detector in some organizations).

In this case, you and the instructor will make inferences about your stress levels during the next 20-30 minutes, based on what the machines say about what is going on inside you. You'll be asked, he explains to you, to reduce your stress levels for about five minutes, then to raise your stress levels for about five minutes, then to lower your stress levels again for about 10 minutes.

Meanwhile, you'll be replying to questions from the instructor concerning the course content. And, to top it off, he'll be *grading* you on both components of the exam: your ability to shape your stress levels and your ability to answer the questions on course content.

Sounds ridiculous, doesn't it?

Well, this is the kind of exam I gave undergraduate and graduate students for many years. Students were almost invariably successful in getting through with distinction.

It wasn't so bad. In fact, it was an uplifting, even inspiring, experience for many students. The performance exam was a major focus of those courses, from the very first meeting. We'd practice all semester. By the time the performance exam arrived, students were accomplished stress shapers.

The students learned to shape stress under very difficult – albeit contrived – circumstances. And that was the point. *Anybody* can shape stress (with just a little instruction) while lying peacefully alone in bed. But who cares?

The issue is: *Can you shape your stress profile and yet engage fully – remain thoroughly immersed – in one of the most stressful occupations yet invented? Can you teach* ***and*** *shape your stress profile at the same time? If you want to maintain your energy levels and high performance, you'll have to.*

That's why I concocted that sadistic-sounding "performance examination" process while I was teaching undergraduate and graduate students in three different university settings over a period of nearly 20 years. I wanted those students – many of them teachers or prospective teachers – to get so accomplished, during a semester with me, at shaping stress *while under pressure,* that they would be able to experience the thrill of performing exceptionally well intellectually while performing exceptionally well psychophysiologically. And, with only occasional exceptions, they did.

Biofeedback and Self-Regulation

You don't need a biofeedback machine to become an outstanding shaper of your own stress profile. But I'd like you to know a couple of things about those devices and what we've learned from them.

When you're in action – that is, nearly all the time – your stress levels are never stable. You're continually, second-to-second, moving up or down the stress scale.

Sometimes you are clearly – maybe painfully – aware of your stress level. You "feel" it in numerous ways. The deep breaths and trembling fingers just after a narrowly averted car accident. The pounding in your chest during an angry confrontation with a parent or student, or just before a scheduled public-speaking engagement. Or, at the opposite end of the stress spectrum, the deep sense of large-muscle relaxation while nodding off in a warm living room on a winter evening.

But moment to moment, few people have any real sense of where their stress level is. Good biofeedback machines show precisely what's happening in the stress systems. For example, a thermal biofeedback device, monitoring your systems by means of a finger plythysmograph, indicates your fingertip surface temperature in hundredths of a degree Fahrenheit.

So what? With second-to-second alterations in your stress level, the little capillaries just under the surface of your fingertips widen and narrow continually. This is known as vasodilation or vasoconstriction, respectively. Thus, with vasodilation – the instantaneous result of a lessening stress level – more warm blood is passing just under the skin surface, and the finger-surface temperature will reflect that in hundredths of a degree Fahrenheit. With vasoconstriction (rising stress level), the opposite will occur.

You see what's happening. This is one tiny piece of the stress response. Your physiology, not "knowing" the difference between threat in the form of your walking to the front of your class to start a lesson, and threat in the form of walking to the front of your cave to confront a physical danger a few millennia ago, engages the fight-or-flight response routinely, every day of your life.

In this thermal biofeedback example I'm using, the fingertip surface capillaries are closing as you walk to the front of the class – *whether you "feel" stressed or not* – because your nervous and other systems interpret your mental activity as signaling an imminent potential threat to your physical well-being. Surface capillaries close down. Blood is diverted to larger muscles, partly to supply more oxygen to those fighting muscles and partly to reduce the quantity of blood flowing near the skin surface in the event you are gashed in the impending attack.

Another biofeedback device called an electromyograph can measure, via electrical signals, the muscle tension present in any muscle or muscle system large enough to accept the device's sensors. Part of your stress response involves your automatic, unthinking tensing of muscle systems in reaction to the next presumed physical attack.

So you often become aware, at the end of the drive home after school, that your shoulder/back muscle system (the trapezius system) actually aches from hours of constant tension. This is muscle tension which began when you walked to the front of your class at 8:00 a.m., which imperceptibly increased as you taught throughout the day, and which was probably exacerbated still further by traffic conditions during the drive home.

Tomorrow, as you drive home, and as you sit immobile at a traffic signal, check on your trapezius system. Can you drop your shoulders? How far? Half an inch? A quarter of an inch?

Most of us are really quite "good" at carrying high levels of muscle tension – another piece of the overall stress response – with us wherever we go, preparing ourselves for physical combat where (with thankfully rare exceptions) that kind of threat is not present.

So it is that biofeedback can be very informative. These machines can do superior jobs of heightening any individual's awareness of her or his habitual responses to stress, both to routine, thousands-of-times-a-day stressors and to the less frequent, usually more noticeable kind. But I'm not here to sell you a piece of equipment. I simply want you to have an idea of the ways in which stress-related research can work, so that you will be better prepared for what comes next.

Alarm Systems and "Shaping" Responses

I used to be scared to show the schematic on the opposite page to an audience. Somehow I expected the group to get up and walk out. In those instances, I was guilty of underestimating the people who had come to learn about stress shaping, performance, and health.

What I actually found, and continue to find, is that audiences want copies of the thing. People want to understand the psychophysiology of stress, and, in the case of audiences of school professionals, want to be quite clear on what is going on inside them as they prepare for and move through each school day.

So, take a look.

Schematic of relationships among:
the somatic nervous system (SNS), the autonomic nervous system (ANS), and the endocrine system (ES)

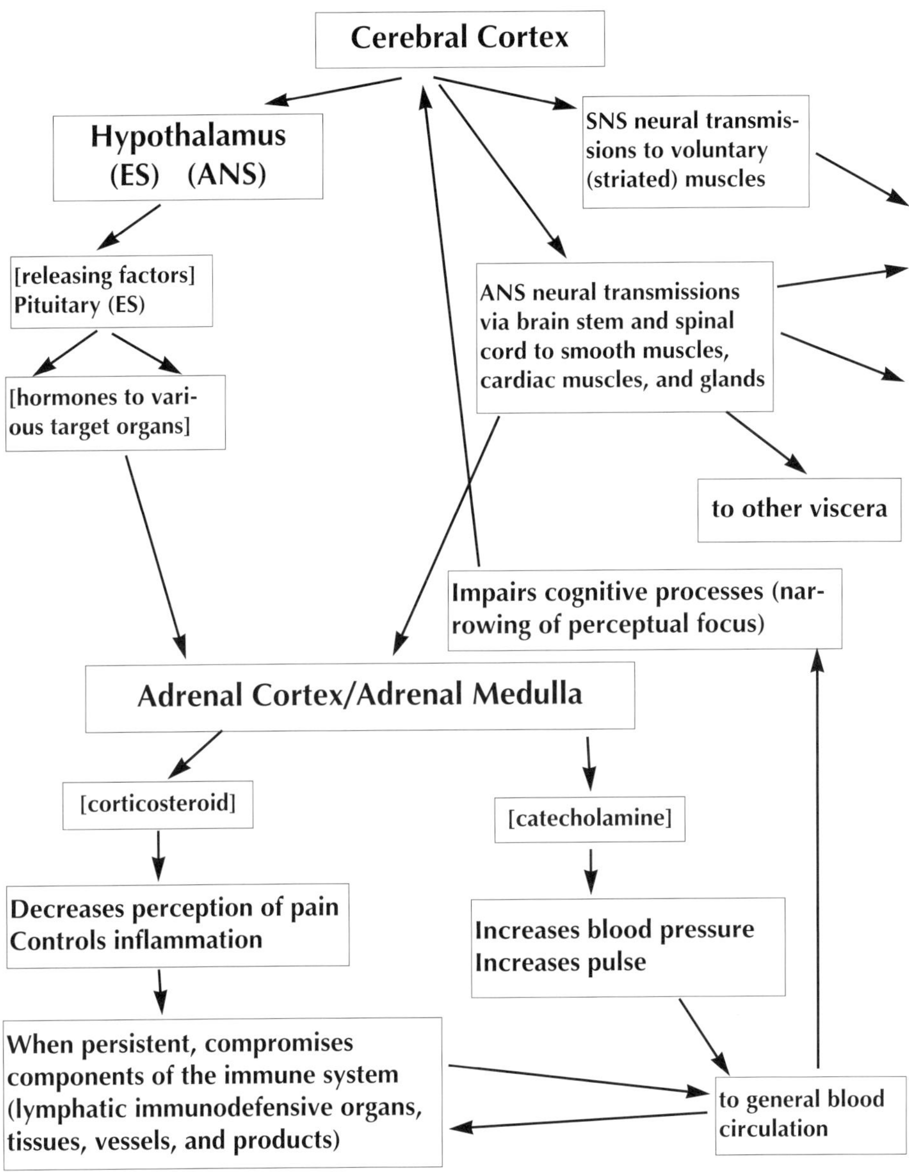

NOTE: This schematic represents some of the most significant relationships among the somatic nervous system, the autonomic nervous system, and the endocrine system. Actual SNS-ANS-ES complexity far exceeds that shown here.

You see the starting point for everything: cerebral cortex. You perceive, you plan, you present, you direct your actions – and, depending upon how you interpret your students' responses, or on how you predict or imagine your students may respond – your body may or may not send neural signals of threat. If there are any "threat messages" whatsoever, including threat messages so small that you haven't the slightest conscious idea that one is in process, some "piece" of the stress response will go into action. And the fact is that in teaching, these low-level threat messages are, for most of us, continual.

Notice, as your eyes follow the arrows down the schematic page just preceding, how *the stress response separates broadly into two categories: one category, generally covering the lower left-hand side of the page, applies to your health; the other category, generally covering the lower right-hand side of the page, applies to your teaching performance.* This unwitting, accidentally self-destructive attack on yourself is led by two categories of hormones, each of which, in more primitive eras, helped humankind survive.

Corticosteroid (`cor-ti-co-`stair-oid). This category of hormone, released in response to the continual "threat messages" originating in your cerebral cortex, does good things for you – provided you are trying to run from one side of the interstate to the other at rush hour. That is, it acts to diminish your perception of pain, and it acts to help control inflammation from physical injury. In short, it helps you continue to function no matter how physically damaged you may be.

What does it do for you while you are teaching? Nothing. Unless you're actually being damaged physically in a fist fight with your students, a parent, or a colleague. But if this corticosteroid remains in your blood stream for a while, as it frequently does during the school day when you've got to be "on" from minute to minute, expect it to do something unwelcome: compromise your immune system's ability to fight disease.

This is not good.

This means you are susceptible to "catching" something your immune system would, if it were at full strength, handle with ease. This is one of the reasons it is so hard to stay healthy as a teacher, year-round. It's not just that the kids come to school with airborne and surface-borne "bugs." It's that your persistently elevated stress levels lead you to maintain higher corticosteroid levels than the ideal, and that, in turn, leads to reduction in your immune system's ability to fight back.

This is not even medically controversial any more. It's just basic stuff.

Please don't misquote me. I didn't say stress causes sickness. I said, in my best "Psychophysiology 101" manner, that one piece of the stress response has the unwanted side effect of reducing your capacity to ward off disease. And stress is, therefore, a major but *indirect* cause of disease.

Catecholamine (`cat-uh-`cole-uh-meen). This category of hormone, also released in response to the series of "threat messages" emanating from your cerebral cortex while you teach (and while you anticipate teaching), also does great things for you – provided, as before, that you are facing an actual fist fight, or sprinting away from a woolly mammoth at top speed.

As the schematic shows, "threat messages" eventually trace a neural and endocrine trail to the adrenal medulla, from which catecholamine is released. Flowing through your blood stream, catecholamines (which include the famous hormone adrenaline) drive both pulse and blood pressure upward in anticipation that your muscles will need a rush of energy-and-strength-supplying oxygen and nutrients so that you'll "fight" or "flee" successfully.

Nothing internally terrible is going on yet, though ... your cardiovascular system is just pounding. Unless you have advanced heart disease, your systems will tolerate these alarms without the ship going under.

Ah, but when these raging catecholamines reach your brain – a matter of only a few seconds – then you find yourself thinking and behaving strangely. Your brain is being prepared to function at its most bestial, its least civilized, its absolute stupidest level.

Your brain has become a yes-or-no decision-making device. It is led to think in terms no more sophisticated than this: "Shall I attack? Or shall I run away?" "Can I kill this threat? Or can it kill me?" "Can I outrun this threat? Or can it outrun me?"

This is why, in confrontations, you never think of the right thing to say until 30 minutes after it's over. This is why, in disciplinary face-offs, you make threats you cannot (or do not really want to) enforce. This is why, in arguments, you blurt out things that later cannot be undone, whether you decide to apologize or not.

This is also why kids "choke" on tests for which they really have studied, why teachers forget what they wanted to say in job interviews, why outraged adults scream obscenities at each other, why cars are driven like weapons.

This is catecholamine.

Final Exam: Psychophysiology 101

Got it, then?

- Threat messages – continual in teaching – trigger electrical and fluid responses inside us.
- In the adrenal gland, two potent classes of hormone are released in response to the threat messages: corticosteroid and catecholamine.
- Corticosteroid, when persistent in the blood stream, reduces the ability of the immune system to fight disease – both "little" and "big" disease.
- Catecholamine, as soon as it arrives in the brain, reduces the ability to think like a sensible human.

That's why this chapter was subtitled "Teaching From the Inside Out," to indicate that, without at least some degree of mastery over these internal events, most of us will have immense difficulty, over the long haul, staying healthy and performing in interactions with kids and parents in the ways we would like.

That said, I now want to take you swiftly through four chapters in which I give you the best, most easily used, and most readily implemented stressor-shaping and stress-shaping strategies and techniques available for classroom and at-home use.

Chapter 8

Shaping the Stressors: Your Stressor Calendar

We all face our share of responsibilities and demands – some from ourselves, some from others. Some of these limitations we can't – or won't – do much about. Others, we can – or might – adjust. The purpose of this chapter is to invite you to think systematically about that. This chapter is about your stressors, the "limitations" placed upon you – and the steps you can take to reduce their negative effects on your health and performance.

You *can* do something about "Psychophysiology 101" – Chapter 7's presentation of the health-and-performance bad news brought on by your daily teaching challenges. You can:

- shape the stressors, the "things" that impinge on you from the outside – such as your teaching or special events schedules; or
- shape your cognitive habits, the mental approaches and responses you customarily make to those stressors; or
- shape your physical responses, the internal neurological and hormonal approaches and responses you customarily make to those stressors; or
- shape what I call the "core system," your cardiovascular system's ability to meet daily physical demands; or
- do several or even all of the above, in various combinations with each other.

In this chapter, we'll look at the first item in that list.

The Social Readjustment Rating Scale

The Holmes and Rahe Social Readjustment Rating Scale[1] is that list of life events from which you assign yourself points based upon which of the listed items you've actually experienced in the past 12 months. After you add them to arrive at your total, you're told that you have (consequently) a certain percentage probability of getting sick in the medium-term future. This Readjustment Scale contains items such as divorce, change of jobs, taking on a new mortgage, getting married, and so on. It also has – this always fascinates people who see it for the first time – "good" events, such as "vacation."

The Holmes and Rahe Scale is old now and not much used, and you can see why. Statistically true or not, it implies that merely because statistical samples of people with point totals ***a***, ***b***, or ***c*** do fall ill, you have probability ***x***, ***y***, or ***z***, of falling ill yourself. It does not take into account your ability, or lack of ability, to handle a given stressor or cluster of stressors. It implies you are only a potential victim in a process.

The Holmes and Rahe Scale does not account for the fact that, for some people an event like a vacation can be stressful, but for others, the same vacation can be truly relaxing. This can be a function of how you handle yourself on the vacation, or it can be that fact coupled with your family's habits and expectations. If you are the person who, by long-standing family habit, organizes the vacation, takes the responsibility for the details, wipes the kids' noses, and does laundry in mid-vacation, and if you continue to accept that role, there may be little about "vacation" which can fall into the category of personal renewal and rejuvenation for you.

No matter. On the Social Readjustment Rating Scale, you're going to get the same 13 points as the rest of your family.

Those are the reasons why people don't like – and don't very often use – the Social Readjustment Rating Scale.

But Holmes and Rahe, and numerous members of the research community before and after them, were onto a very useful, relevant, signifi-

---

[1] Holmes, T., and Rahe, R., "The Social Readjustment Rating Scale," *Journal of Psychosomatic Research*, 11:213-18.

significant idea: *The quantity and quality of stressors you experience in a given unit of time correlate powerfully with your (predicted) stress level and its effects (via corticosteroid) upon your immune system's capacity to ward off disease.* In addition, although harder to measure, it is almost certainly true as well that *those same stressors-per-time-unit correlate with the effects of stress on your* ***performance*** *as a teacher (via catecholamine).*

Back in Chapter 2, "Long Odds and The Big Picture," I displayed for you Dr. Hans Selye's General Adaptation Syndrome, followed by the Selye-Snelling Stress Curves, followed by the Center for Teacher Renewal's pilot study curves: curves showing estimated teacher performance, enthusiasm, and stress for a school-year cycle. Those curves, showing performance/enthusiasm/stress deterioration during certain parts of the school year, support the Holmes and Rahe Scale's implications in one respect and, paradoxically, support one of the criticisms of that scale in another respect. That is: (1) stressors tend to affect teachers in predictable ways; and (2) teachers can do something to "shape their responses" to those stressors (because, in some studied schools, you'll remember, the "curves" were flat).

A Summary Stressor Calendar

To encourage you to begin to think in "stressor-shaping" terms, I've supplied you with a Summary Stressor Calendar. On the next two pages, you'll see, on the left-hand page, an explanation of the Calendar's use, and, on the right-hand page, the Calendar itself.[2]

2 I am indebted to my colleague, Mr. Donald W. Fudge, both for his development of the "calendar circle" idea (applied by him in the school-*management* context), and for his endorsement of this extensive adaptation of the circle for these purposes.

Summary Stressor Calendar

Grab a pencil.

Find the circle, near the center of the calendar, labeled "A." You see from the legend that "A" refers to your "School Calendar" for the year. Follow that circle around the 360 degrees, stopping at each month to write a number, one through four, to represent the estimated (and/or predicted) level of stressors you face in that month, *just from school-related stressors* – such as the surge of paperwork at the end of grading periods, or the time demands of the annual drama production, which you have co-directed for years. The lower-right scale defines the ratings (e.g., "1" indicates "low-level stressors"). This takes about three minutes.

That finished, move outward from the center to the circle labeled "B," the one dealing with your "Family Calendar" for the year. Repeat the previous process, this time thinking only of *family-related stressors* – such as your kids' moving up to a new school, or the trek to the annual family reunion.

Continue through bands "C," "D," "E," and "F." (Leave band "G" blank for a minute; I'll come back to it.) Bear in mind that merely because a given month may have no "happenings" of note, IT MAY STILL CONSTITUTE A HIGH-LEVEL STRESSOR MONTH WITHIN A PARTICULAR BAND. Some of you are in classrooms or in families that consistently provide you with months of "high-level stressors," even *without* a "happening" such as the end of a grading period or your co-directing the drama production. Be as accurate as you can in all six bands and in all 12 months. This can tell you a lot about why you feel the way you feel as each school year develops.

When you finish, sum each month's stressor ratings, and write your monthly totals in the unlabeled interior band, near the Calendar's center (*see sample filled-in Calendar, page 95*). Unless you have skipped one of the bands, you'll write at least a "6" in each month's summary space.

Summary Stressor Calendar

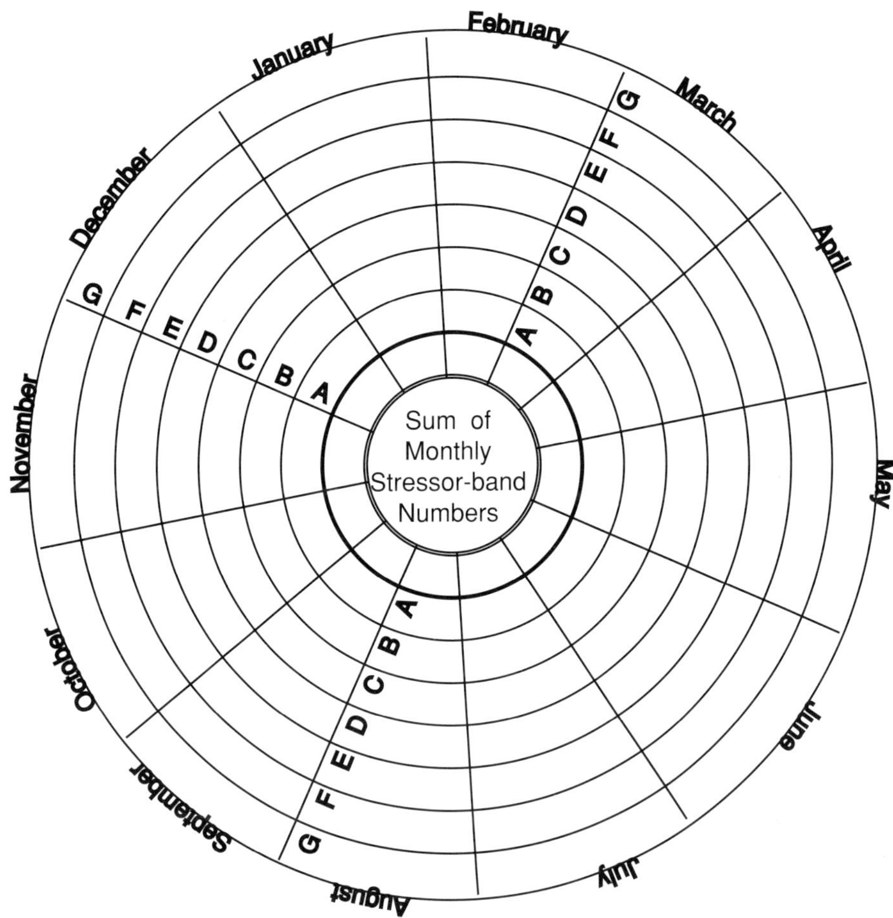

Legend:

Seven Stressor Bands	Stressor Rating Scale, Bands A-G*
A. School Calendar	1. Low-level stressors
B. Family Calendar	2. Mid-level stressors
C. Community Service Calendar	3. High-level stressors
D. Special Events Calendar	4. Very high-level stressors
E. Social Events Calendar	
F. Religious (and other) Holidays Calendar	
G. Unplanned/Emergency Events Calendar	

* Please note: stressor ratings refer both to quantity and quality. Thus, "high-level" can refer to a large number of minor stressors, or to a smaller number of large stressors.

Your arithmetical maximum for a given month is 24, a sum you'll get if you decide you face "very high-level stressors" – worth four points each – for each of the six types of stressors faced in a particular month.

Finally, imagine what would happen in each of the 12 months, should you encounter "unplanned/emergency" stressors (band "G"). Note that your "6s" might become "9s" or "10s," and your "18s" might become "21s" or "22s."

A Sample Filled-in Stressor Calendar

The facing page shows a sample filled-in Stressor Calendar. In this example, the fact that the imaginary teacher is the mother of school-aged children causes her "A-band" and "B-band" to mirror each other's fluctuations. Her School Calendar higher-stressor months tend to be the same as her Family Calendar higher-stressor months, due to her parental involvement with her children's school.

The example's monthly totals, rank-ordered from highest-stressor month to lowest-stressor month, read as follows:

(1) December – 21 total stressor-points;

(2) May – 18 points;

(3) November – 16 points;

(4) April – 14 points;

(5) September – 13 points;

(6) March – 11 points;

(7, 8) June and August – 10 points each;

(9, 10) January and February – 9 points each;

(11, 12) July and October – 8 points each.

The example person's average monthly score is 12.25. Her median monthly score is 10.5.

A Sample Filled-in Stressor Calendar

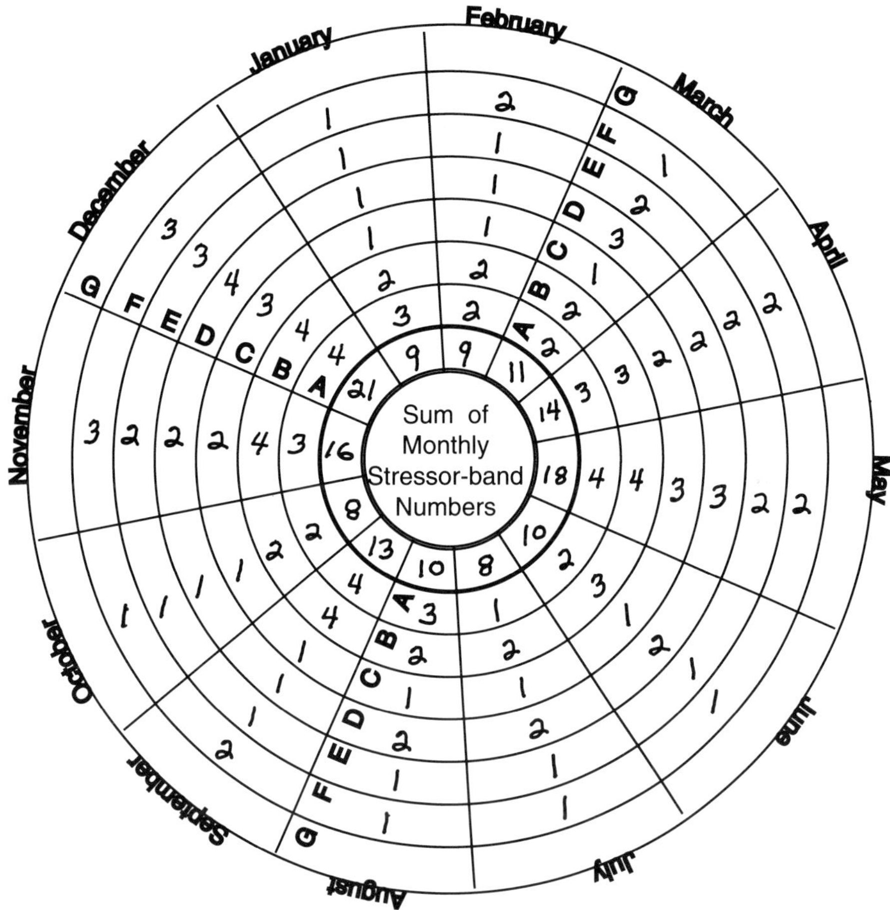

Top Three Stressor Months

1. December
2. May
3. November

Stressor Bands Most Susceptible to Stressor Shaping

1. "D"/Special Events
2. "E"/Social Events
3. ________________

continued next page

Numerical Goals for Top Three Stressor Months, in Most Susceptible Bands

December: 2 (from current 4 in Band "D,", Special Events)

December: 2 (from current 3 in Band "E,", Social Events)

May: 2 (from current 3 in Band "D,", Special Events)

May: 1 (from current 2 in Band "E," Social Events)

November: 1 (from current 2 in Band "D," Special Events)

November: 1 (from current 2 in Band "E," Social Events)

Resulting Summary Numerical Goals for Top Three Stressor Months

1. December: 18 (from current 21)
2. May: 16 (from current 18)
3. November: 14 (from current 16)

What would I recommend for this teacher?

- I would ask her to circle every number on her calendar over which she has some stressor-shaping control, that is, some capacity and willingness to make changes in her customary, habitual "obligations."
- If she cannot – or is unwilling to – influence stressors in the A-band, then she'll mark her highest-stressor School Calendar months for special stress-shaping attention as she reads the rest of *High-Energy Teaching*.
- If she decides that she can "shape" stressors in – let's say – bands "C" through "F," then she'll consider ways in which she might influence events in her Community Service Calendar, her Special Events Calendar, her Social Events Calendar, and her Religious (and other) Holidays Calendar.
- Having decided, let's say, that she not only can influence events in two of those four – her Special Events Calendar and her Social Events Calendar – but is actually willing to do so, then I would sug-

gest that she write down her plan. How, exactly, will she be more assertive with people – some of them family members – who are accustomed to her playing a lead role in all Special Events, and who are accustomed, as well, to her attendance at a variety of Social Events throughout the year? What are the likely consequences of saying no? How can she do a responsible job of redefining others' expectations of her?

- Once she has worked out a written plan for her approach to stressor shaping in the two areas of Special Events and Social Events, I would recommend that she start with the months showing the highest point totals – December, May, and November, in her case – and write down what seems to her the specific application, in those three months, of her more general (year-round) stressor-shaping process. Thereby, she forms an explicit plan of action to shape the stressors in those two bands, in those three months.
- I'd suggest she conclude this segment of her stressor-shaping plans by returning to her filled-in Stressor Calendar, to pencil in her newly developed numerical goals in bands "D" and "E" – Special Events and Social Events. She will examine her December Special Events schedule, we'll imagine, and decide that she is willing to forego, or to play a reduced leadership role in, her club's annual December fund-raising projects. And she will examine her December Social Events schedule, we'll also imagine, and decide that, of the four open houses and two dinners to which she and her husband are often invited, she is willing to negotiate with him to cut the total in half. Her newly developed numerical goals for her three highest-stressor months may, by the time she finishes her plans, drop from an actual or predicted 4, 3, and 2 (band "D" for December, May, and November, respectively) to, I would hope, a 2, 2, and 1 (band "D" for those same highest-stressor months for her). Her numbers in band "E" may have dropped from 3, 2, and 2, to 2, 1, and 1, respectively. She would then compute, in her interior Calendar ring, her new "Sum of Monthly Stressor-band Numbers" for her three toughest months.
- Together, she and I would then look at her new monthly stressor-point sums. December will have dropped from 21 to 18; May, from 18 to 16; and November, from 16 to 14. Her annual self-estimated,

monthly stressor average will drop from 12.25 to 11.7. (Her previous median of 10.5 will not be affected by the changes shown in this example.)

Would that smallish numerical shift make any difference? YES.

In real-world stressor shaping, small numerical changes on your Stressor Calendar usually result in real, "felt" differences, as you actually pass through the months in question. I really want to emphasize this.

Getting any of your monthly single-band numbers to go down even a single point, usually makes a perceptible difference in how you feel through the month. This is especially true if you're dealing with your highest-stressor months. Moving a 22 to a 21 matters. Moving a 19 to an 18 matters. (Moving a very low-stressor month down a point – say, an 8 to a 7 – may not matter much at all.) This is why I urge you to start with your highest-stressor months. Install those changes right away, if you possibly can.

If this hypothetical (but not unusual) teacher can make stressor-shaping progress with her Special Events Calendar and her Social Events Calendar in December, May, and November, then she gives herself a chance to be healthier, to feel stronger, to perform better in the classroom, and to advance her own personal/professional renewal program.

If I were working with this imaginary teacher, I'd ask her to consider showing her filled-in Stressor Calendar to family members, including her fairly young children. She might even invite them to do their own Stressor Calendars. Her family might develop some real insight into why there are certain times during the year when family members have all kinds of interpersonal problems with each other and with others, and when they tend to get colds and other annoying minor sicknesses, too.

She'll need to be clear with them, as I have tried to be in this chapter, on the difference between stress<u>or</u> shaping, which the Stressor Calendar addresses, and stress shaping, which we will examine in the next three chapters.

On the facing page is a blank Stressor Calendar for your own use. For assistance in filling out the calendar, you may decide to first answer the worksheet questions that begin on page 100.

Your Summary Stressor Calendar

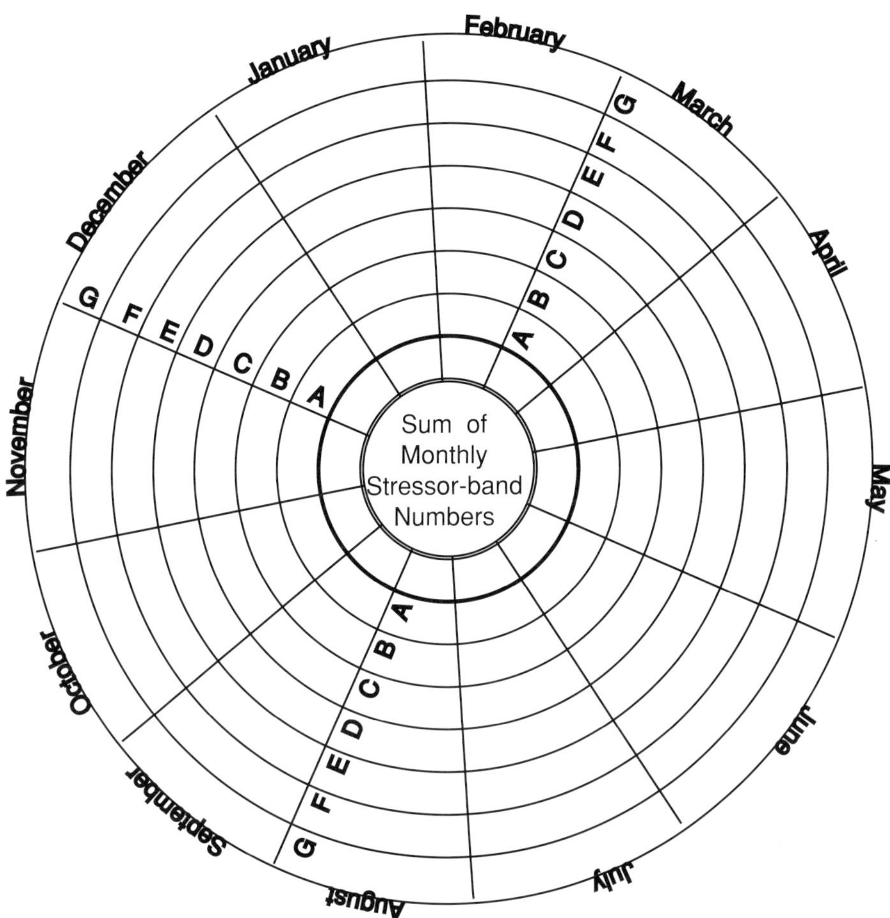

Top Three Stressor Months

1. ______________________________
2. ______________________________
3. ______________________________

Stressor Bands Most Susceptible to Stressor Shaping

1. ______________________________
2. ______________________________
3. ______________________________

Numerical Goals for Top Three Stressor Months, in Most Susceptible Bands

____

____

____

____

____

____

Resulting Summary Numerical Goals for Top Three Stressor Months

____

____

____

Summary Stressor Calendar: A Worksheet

For assistance in filling out the Summary Stressor Calendar on the preceding page, you may choose to do some writing in response to the questions following.

1. In which of the Stressor Bands ("A" through "F") do I most need to do stressor shaping?____________________

   ____

   ____

   ____

2. In which of the Stressor Bands am I most willing – and in the best position – to do stressor shaping? ____________________

   ____

   ____

   ____

3. Exactly how might I approach – or respond to – individuals in my targeted Bands (presumably those listed in #2), in order to redefine their expectations of me, in the most appropriately assertive manner? ____

____

____

____

____

____

____

____

____

____

____

The Dreaded Band "G"

Now, a few words about band "G," the one I called "Unplanned/ Emergency Events Calendar." Earlier, I asked you to imagine how any entry in that band would affect the arithmetic of your monthly summary figures for the Stressor Calendar. In the example we've worked with, a high-stress, unplanned entry in December would have added three unwanted points to our imaginary teacher's already astronomical total of 21. What would her chances be of getting through a 24-point-stressor month with teaching job, family life, other responsibilities, and her health and sanity still in one piece?

Not great.

The way to plan for the unplanned is to prioritize your Stressor Bands now, while no unplanned/emergency conditions exist. Our sample teacher, under imaginary "normal" conditions, was willing to attack bands "D" and "E" only. But I would want her to think beyond that, and to imagine a three-point addition to each month on her Stressor Calendar.

Three more December points gives her 24. Three more May points gives her 21. Three more August points moves a fairly low-stressor month, on her calendar, to one which is above-average stressor level for her.

I'd want her to prioritize her bands, month by month, through all 12 months, given the addition of a three-point unplanned stressor to each. Beyond her chosen bands, "D" and "E," which bands would she then attack further? Would bands "C" and "F" become fair game with a three-point unplanned stressor addition to band "G?" If so, in which months? All 12? Or only some?

I'd want her to look again at the Stressor Calendar Worksheet, where she wrote scenarios to follow in asking others to redefine their expectations of her in particular bands. I'd ask her to think of new scenarios to follow with bands which she is currently unwilling to attack, but might be, given a high enough stressor load in a given month.

Planning for the unplanned is not nonsense. It's what we teach our children to do all the time.

Gratuitous Reminder

My closing gratuitous reminder: This chapter has dealt only with stressor shaping. As I wrote at chapter's start, everybody I've ever known has responsibilities and demands placed upon him or her. Some of those limitations cannot be realistically attacked ("shaped"). Others can be. This chapter has invited you to think systematically about shaping those that you can and will adjust.

I'll turn now to psychology and physiology, and the approaches and techniques that allow you to shape stress within yourself. But regardless of how involved you may get with the upcoming material in Chapters 9, 10, and 11, don't let go of what you've planned to do in order to shape your stress<u>ors</u>.

There is no virtue in stacking the deck against yourself. Shape whatever stressors you possibly can. Give your mind and body a fighting chance.

Chapter 9

Shaping the Cognitive Habits: Ritual Reflection

Want to experience an hour of great fun and *astounding* inspiration? Watch and listen to Guy Doud, former national Teacher of the Year, on videotape.[1]

My favorite part of the video presentation is Guy's description of his own sixth-grade teacher, Norm Card. It seems that Mr. Card was the first teacher to begin to re-route some of young Guy's cognitive habits. (Guy doesn't talk that way about it. I do.)

Guy says that one of the first things he learned when he started school as a child was that he was fat. That hadn't occurred to him previously. His whole family was fat. He thought that was how you were supposed to look. His peers let him know right away, of course, that he was wrong about that. And wrong about a lot of other things, too. Guy learned he was different. He learned he was odd. He learned he would always be picked last when the kids chose teams at recess. He learned his place on the socio-economic ladder: very low (something that was obvious from the size of his six-crayon box, in contrast to a classmate's 64-crayon box, complete with sharpener on the back). He learned essentially that he wasn't any good, that he was poor, that he was fat. Guy hated school and thought little more than that of himself.

Then came Mr. Card.

Mr. Card let Guy know that he regarded him as an able young per-

---

1 Available from Focus on the Family Films, Pomona, CA (714-620-8588). changed to 719/531-5181

son. And when the class went out to recess, Mr. Card himself picked the teams. And beyond that, Mr. Card actually engaged this unpopular, overweight, odd young man in conversation from time to time, treating him with the same respect he accorded other, more popular, more athletic, more conventional, skinnier youngsters in the classroom.

Guy remembers Mr. Card announcing to the class that he and Mrs. Card were expecting their first child. And he remembers Mr. Card bringing the baby to class for all the kids to see.

And finally, at year's end, Mr. Card, *who was in his first year of teaching,* told the kids that he did not want to forget his first class, so he had pasted individual snapshots of each student into a big, red scrapbook. Mr. Card circulated the scrapbook and asked each one of those sixth-graders to write something beside his or her own picture.

After Guy was presented with the national Teacher of the Year award by then-President Ronald Reagan, Guy returned to his Midwest teaching venue, to be greeted ceremoniously by a long string of dignitaries from the state level on down. As he and his wife stepped from the plane, and as he surveyed this imposing line of people, his eyes fastened on a familiar figure at the very end of the line. Mr. Card was waiting.

Red scrapbook under his arm.

Guy ran past the governor, the commissioner of education, the mayor, the superintendent of schools, his principal, and the other Important People, to embrace Mr. Card, the Teacher of the Year's Prime Mover.

Then, together, Mr. Card and Guy Doud examined the red scrapbook. And there, scrawled next to the photo of an odd, overweight, shaved-head kid, was this message:

Dear Mr. Card,

Thank you for being so nice to me.

Guy Doud

Cognitive Habits

"Cognitive habits" doesn't sound like it has anything to do with emotions, with old wounds, with Prime Movers, with anything even remotely "spiritual." Am I right?

The fact is, the topic of cognitive habits has everything to do with the deepest, most powerful forces that lie within each person. Which is why I urge you to create time for "Ritual Reflection" and recommitment to your vocation.

I'm convinced that *it is naive for us to assume that we can enter into any long-term, emotionally-rooted endeavor – such as marriage, such as a deep religious commitment, such as our fundamental commitments to our children and to our parents – without the regularly reinforcing, ritually evocative behaviors necessary to sustain the endeavor, the commitment, or the relationship.*

Think about it. In any long-term, *successful,* loving relationship you've had, recall how you both developed everyday ways of reinforcing the spirit of commitment with which the two of you began your journey together. Some of those everyday expressions were subtle mannerisms, such as a certain smile or a peck on the cheek, while others were more explicit, such as a spoken "I love you." But if the relationship was really successful, there were surely a number of regularly invoked "ritual behaviors," "ritual phrases," and instances of "ritual reflection" in which you both engaged. And the successful result of those rituals was to *help you keep alive the meaning of the original commitment.*

Of course, rituals can lose their meaning, if you allow them to. To invoke your rituals successfully, you made sure that those rituals did not lose meaning for you. You regularly practiced *meaningful* evocation of your original commitment.

Now – apply that idea to your vocation.

I believe that many teachers enter the profession with a profound sense, or at least a profound *hope,* that teaching is the very best thing they can do with their lives. In the process of turning that powerful inner sense, that resonant hope, into action, teachers develop a set of expectations – a particular way of looking at the world of schooling.

Early on, when this inner sense, this resonant hope, is strongest, *many teachers are at their emotional, commitment-focused best at the same time that they are technically at their weakest.* Guy Doud's sixth-grade teacher, Mr. Card, is an example of a young teacher at his emotional, commitment-focused best.

Mr. Card may or may not have been technically weak in that first year of his teaching career. But, technically weak or technically strong or technically evolving, he brought an inner sense of hope, of high expectations, and of a kind of spiritual excitement to that classroom. And that emotional, commitment-focused sense of hope was inevitably and powerfully communicated to those young people.

Judging from the emotion on Guy Doud's face (on the videotape) when he describes seeing Mr. Card on the occasion of the Teacher of the Year's triumphant return home, we can sense the depth of Guy's gratitude. And we can assume that young Guy was not the only youngster similarly affected by the *spirit of commitment* Mr. Card brought to his sixth-grade classroom.

And we can guess, finally, that Mr. Card's development over the years of a fine repertoire of teaching technique never led him to relinquish his original spirit of commitment. If he had, that red scrapbook would probably have stayed at the bottom of a box, at the bottom of a stack of other boxes, in the remotest corner of the attic.

I do not know Mr. Card. But I'd like to think that he has a similar scrapbook for each class of kids he has taught over the decades, and that he pauses regularly for Ritual Reflection, focusing in part on the parade of young lives that he affected (and which, of course, affected Mr. Card in return). I'd like to think that he draws further inspiration from such Ritual Reflection. I'd like to think that this sort of focused reminiscence helps give him purpose, an expanded sense of hope, a broadened sense of high expectations, and a powerful sense of spiritual excitement as he moves into his classroom every single Monday, Tuesday, Wednesday, Thursday, and Friday morning.

And I'd like to think Mr. Card understands that this kind of commitment requires *purposeful attention and nourishment* as do all other major, passionate commitments that human beings make in their lifetimes.

Ritual Reflection Revisited

Sixty minutes of Ritual Reflection each month is, I believe, a realistic way for most of you to revisit and refocus your original inner direction and sense of purpose, without in any way sacrificing the technical competence you have developed with such effort and determination.

But Ritual Reflection and its consequences – this recapturing of First Purposes – is never convenient. And its implications may turn out to be inconvenient, also.

The more your First Purposes become part of a reshaped set of cognitive habits (as you consider your classroom), the less TIDY things tend to become. Kids may start to slip out of their pigeon holes. A creeping subjectivity may seep into your grading system. Your punishment approaches may become increasingly idiosyncratic, changing from kid to kid, and from incident to incident.

Is that good?

Well, I don't pretend to know. I can't tell you how you ought to teach. I can just tell you that, *unless you recover some of what drove you to this vocation originally, you will not be as psychologically, emotionally, spiritually, or physically strong and alive as you ought to be for your own sake and, indirectly, for the sake of everybody with whom you interact at school, at home, and in the community.*

The chart on the next page is a good place to begin.

Ritual Reflection Chart I: First Purposes

Use this chart to help organize your Ritual Reflection time, and as a log-keeping device to track your progress as you rekindle your First Purposes as an educator. Be sure to adapt both the chart itself and its usage to fit your needs, your professional/personal context, and your Professional Development Plan (Chapter 5).

Names of Prime Movers From My Past

Elementary levels________________________________

Middle grade levels________________________________

High school levels________________________________

College/grad school levels________________________________

Some of my Prime Movers' characteristics________________________________

____

First Purposes: a summary of factors that drew me to the profession

____

____

____

Current state of my First Purposes (from preceding list)

____

____

____

Thoughts about the "current state of my First Purposes" (from preceding list)

____

____

____

Plans and progress notes: recovering "the spirit of purpose"

____

____

____

____

____

____

I recommend 60 minutes a month. This should be a solid time block, not two half-hour or four quarter-hour sessions.

Where should your Ritual Reflection be done? Probably not at school, unless you want to place it at the very end of a particular day every month, at a time of day when the building is mostly empty and you *can be certain of an uninterrupted time for* **this**. Trying to do *a meaningful* Ritual Reflection in your classroom before the school day starts, or during your "free" time within the school day, is a mistake for most teachers. Your mind is too full, your motor is running too fast, your sense of time urgency is too great. Do this at the very end of a school day, or at home. You decide.

Just keep in mind that you'll need to be truly focused on this, or it will become just another set of idle, day-dreaming minutes in your life. *Cognitive habits and all the related internal events that accompany them – core emotions, basic commitments, fundamental motivating drives – shift gradually but surely in response to this kind of ritual commitment, taken seriously, and accompanied by log-keeping activity.*

But keep in mind my earlier caveat. Making this shift in your thinking a meaningful one takes effort and commitment in itself. This is not a low-grade mental "time-out." It is a serious, self-teaching process.

Attitude Shapers and Ritual Reflection

I'm changing the subject a little now. What you just finished reading about Ritual Reflection and First Purposes is a "teaching unit" in itself. It was the most critical part of this chapter in *High-Energy Teaching*.

There is, however, a related set of ideas that I also want you to have. Bear in mind as you go, though, that this is *supplementary* material. It builds on what you just read. It does not change it, or make it more complicated.

First, before you continue reading in this chapter, I'd like you to decide what you think of Ritual Reflection. I'd like you to make a commitment to working on that absolutely fundamental component in cognitive-habit shaping. *Then*, for further work in the cognitive habit area, I'd like you to give some thought to what I'm about to discuss.

Now ... let me give you these supplemental thoughts, tools and suggestions.

Dr. Albert Ellis is a clinical psychologist, author, and speaker, who for more than 30 years has been at the forefront in the field of cognitive psychology. Years ago, he developed a list of 12 cognitive habits associated with emotional disturbance.

As the years – make that decades – have passed, I've regularly but informally applied Dr. Ellis' list, in teaching and counseling situations, to the people with whom I have worked. Nearly all of those people have been, like you, psychologically "normal."

The following list is mine, but borrows directly and heavily from Ellis' original one. Read through this six-item list thoughtfully, keeping in mind the discussion just completed about Ritual Reflection and First Purposes, and the role of cognitive habits in reforming your most basic attitudes and motives regarding your profession.

Six Attitude Shapers

1. Replace the cognitive habit:

   It is necessary for me to be loved by everybody for everything I do ...

   with this "attitude shaper":

   I'll concentrate more on loving than on being loved.

2. Replace the cognitive habit:

   Certain students (or parents, or colleagues) are beyond help ...

with this "attitude shaper":

I'll focus on shaping these students' (parents/colleagues) attitudes; I'll stay involved with them.

3. Replace the cognitive habit:

   I need to have certain and perfect control over everything ...

   with this "attitude shaper":

   I can learn to live with, and even to view as interesting, the messiness of teaching/learning, with all its inherent probability and chance.

4. Replace the cognitive habit:

   Bad news is catastrophic ...

   with this "attitude shaper":

   Bad news needs to be met with a strategy, preferably one that minimizes the likelihood of a repeat.

5. Replace the cognitive habit:

   I must be thoroughly competent and achieving in all respects ...

   with this "attitude shaper":

   I would be better off to <u>do</u> than to be "perfect."

6. Replace the cognitive habit:

   The past determines my present and future ...

   with this "attitude shaper":

   I can learn from the past and make the future quite different.

This list, obviously, seeks to pair "bad" (impractical, counterproductive, stress-inducing) cognitive habits with "good" (practical, productive, stress-shaping) cognitive habits. Are you thinking, maybe, that the six "attitude shapers" are just plain common sense? Completely obvious to any thinking person?

If so, remind yourself that that's not the question at all. The question is: What are your *cognitive habits*, in regard to those six items? What is your habituated, unthinking response pattern?

Ritual Reflection II: Habituated Thoughts

I've been insistent. And maybe you've mentally agreed with me. You're going to carve out one hour a month for Ritual Reflection and recommitment to your vocation. You have examined the chart titled "Ritual Reflection Chart I: First Purposes," page 108. And you have, I hope, committed to making a serious trial run with Ritual Reflection, focusing on what I call the absolutely critical starting point of cognitive shaping: your First Purposes.

As a supplemental component in your Ritual Reflection process, consider adding to it the cognitive reshaping of your habituated thoughts, using the six-item list you just read. On the pages following is "Ritual Reflection Chart II: Habituated Thoughts." I have filled in this one to give you a feel for it.

A Sample Ritual Reflection Chart II: Habituated Thoughts

Current cognitive habit	Preferred cognitive habit	Reinforcement strategies
1. My students *must* like me	I *must* like my students	a. Focus 3 minutes on each of my top three problem kids during my Ritual Reflection with emphasis on altering the dynamic between us
2. Certain students are beyond help	I can successfully shape my students' attitudes if I stay involved with them	b. Focus 3 minutes on my most recent *successful* interaction with each of these three kids
3. "Immersion" with my students is too emotionally exhausting	"Immersion" with my students is the *only* way I can rejuvenate and renew *myself*	c. Focus 5-20 minutes during each Ritual Reflection on my original rationale for entering the teaching field, and on the emotions and hopes I then knew

Ritual Reflection/Habituated Thoughts Log:

Month one Had a breakthrough with Don; another setback with Rosa; told James I'd give him a ride to karate next month; liked my Ritual Reflection time; thought for a long time after Ritual Reflection about why Prime Movers (Mrs. Brown, Mr. Jackson) affected my life so much; decided to reshape my thinking about Don, Rosa, and James by trying especially hard to catch them doing something right so I can give them more reinforcement.

Month two Liked my Ritual Reflection time again – thought mostly about the "spirit of purpose" I used to have; worked on my cognitive habits, especially my reluctance to plunge in and get involved with Don, Rosa, and James – worked in Ritual Reflection time on getting my mind accustomed to thinking that thought which I know is true (but which I don't act on) – the one in my #2 – "I can successfully shape my students' attitudes if I stay involved with them."

Month three Felt discouraged during my Ritual Reflection time, until I focused again on my Prime Movers and was reminded that there is no renewal "from a distance" – renewed my determination to change the dynamic between me and Don, Rosa, and James; determined to try again to help James through his karate interests; resolved to spend a couple of minutes every day for the next two weeks, reshaping that first cognitive habit (#1, about my concern about being liked) – it's really time to get rid of that one.

Month four Looking back over the last month during Ritual Reflection, I felt really excited by the changes in Don and James; both of them have finally started to respond to my persistence with them; James may even earn an "A" in math if he keeps this up – unbelievable! But I see no progress with Rosa yet. I do sense some progress with myself in reshaping both my "immersion" reluctance AND my over-concern with what students think of me – maybe I can carry that over into other areas of my life, too.

Consider working with Chart I and Chart II in combination. Here is an approach with which you can experiment:

- Set aside 60 minutes a month for your Ritual Reflection.
- During Ritual Reflection, do not just sit and think; *write*.
- Using Chart I ("First Purposes"), page 108, ground yourself in a currently legitimate, mature version of your original *spirit of purpose* in

committing yourself to the teaching profession. *This* is the ESSENTIAL step, and one in which to engage during Ritual Reflection, every month, regardless of whether or not you utilize Chart II.

- Using Chart II ("Habituated Thoughts"), beginning on page 113, examine your cognitive habits, as they relate to your First Purposes (as shown in my example #3 in the partially filled-in Chart II), *and* as those relate to Albert Ellis' list of cognitive habits (as shown in my examples #1 and #2 in the partially filled-in Chart II), and as those relate to any other habituated – and counterproductive – cognitive habits that your Ritual Reflections lead you to confront.
- Having done that, keep a weekly anecdotal record of your progress.

Don't underestimate the importance of the third column in Chart II. Without "reinforcement strategies," cognitive-habit shaping won't happen. In fact, without reinforcement strategies, you might as well stick Chart II on the refrigerator and forget it, because nothing in your *habits* is likely to change.

In my example "reinforcement strategies" column, I showed, among other items, that this imaginary teacher intended to devote three minutes of recollection for each of the three students in question, of previously *successful* interactions with them. As the months pass, those successes will, I hope, become fresh experiences each day. This is a good example of cognitively reinforcing yourself *while* your cognitive habits modify themselves. Take ritual, systematic satisfaction in recalling the interpersonal results of your cognitive-habit changes.

Use your 60-minute Ritual Reflection for planning what you intend to change, and for logging your progress. With your Chart II, page 117, pencil into the first column your current cognitive habit(s). Then, as I demonstrated on the worksheet, pencil into the second column your *preferred* cognitive habit(s). Finally, write out your reinforcement strategies.

Putting Things Together

Now you've worked through "Shaping the Stressors" (Chapter 8) and through "Shaping the Cognitive Habits." You've already put two and two together, and deduced that the Stressor Calendar ought to have a bearing on the two charts in this chapter: "First Purposes" and "Habituated Thoughts."

You're right. My recommendation to you is that, in your highest-stressor months (December, May, and November in Chapter 8's examples), you focus in your Ritual Reflection on Chart I (in this chapter) only, rather than on both Chart I and Chart II.

A major implication of the Stressor Calendar is that you should *simplify* your life as much as possible during your peak stressor periods. In this case, simplification may imply doing only what I have called the most critical component in Ritual Reflection – contemplation of and recommitment to a mature version of your First Purposes (Chart I) – and, probably, letting go of Ritual Reflection's supplementary cognitive activities (Chart II).

As always, I'd like you to make that decision. My purpose here is to remind you that the Stressor Calendar's basic principle – simplification in peak-stressor periods – applies just as much to your Ritual Reflection as it does to everything else in your life.

But however you choose to integrate your Stressor Calendar with the two charts in this chapter, make the integration your own. Just as you would want your students to *understand* two important and related ideas enough to adapt them to each other, I ask you to think through the relationships between your calendar of stressors, on the one hand, and your clusters of cognitive habits, on the other.

Ritual Reflection Chart II: Habituated Thoughts

Current cognitive habit	Preferred cognitive habit	Reinforcement strategies
1. ____	1 ____	a ____
2. ____	2 ____	b ____
3. ____	3 ____	c ____
4. ____	4 ____	d ____
5. ____	5 ____	e ____

Ritual Reflection/Habituated Thoughts Log

Month one ____

Month two____

Month three______________________________________

Month four_______________________________________

Sunday Evenings

Unfortunately, Sunday evenings are followed by Monday mornings. That being the case, you can use Sunday evenings as a thermometer of sorts.

If you take seriously the Stressor Calendar and if you give Ritual Reflection a fair test – let's say four consecutive months of doing Ritual Reflection purposefully for 60 minutes each month – then the "feel" of Sunday evening should start to be a little different.

Do you know what I mean?

Creeping into your Sunday evenings should be a trace of anticipation, a sort of "consciousness smile" that on Monday morning you'll again have the *opportunity* to work with your kids.

I'm not being naive here. I know we'd all prefer no responsibilities at all on Monday mornings. So I don't mean that you should be looking toward a routine Monday morning with the same feeling that you would a relaxing vacation on the beach. But I do mean that, if you're taking seriously the Stressor Calendar's implications and those of your Ritual Reflection activities, Sunday evening should start to feel a little better than it has in the past.

There is no magic in any of these procedures. But, as with the teaching/learning process itself, you can thoroughly reshape how you've come to think and feel about your career, if you *work* at it systematically.

And if you do work at it systematically, and if you sense no reshaping progress at all over a four-month period, and if your assessment of your attitudes is that you cannot retrieve even a shadow of your First Purposes, and that you cannot reshape your daily cognitions in the least – it may be time to move. It may be to a different school. It may be to a different career. But you can only be honest with yourself, and you can only be of meaningful service to kids or to this society, with a carefully nurtured, mature version of the "spirit of commitment" with which you began.

Ritual Reflection, thoughtfully employed, will give you a chance to recapture something you may have unwittingly lost, and which, until now, you may not even have missed.

Contribute
***your own successful examples of Stressor Calendar shaping, First Purposes reminiscence, and Habitual Thoughts shaping to the CTR newsletter,* Teachers in Touch.**

Call 1-800-955-4944

Chapter 10

Shaping the Physical Responses: QR & Counting Down

The most stressing daily school occurrence I know is the little kids' reading group. You know, the one in which the Bluebirds – six elementary children of similar reading ability – sit in a little circle and, when called upon, read a sentence or two from their reading books.

Are you imagining those six little kids? Okay, think about that situation. It has these stress-inducing characteristics:

- The kids have a difficult (for them) task to perform – the *public* translation of a mystifying array of small, black, printed shapes into familiar sounds.
- They will be evaluated on the performance by an authority figure.
- They will be evaluated as well (informally) by their peers.
- They have no control over which part of the performance/task will be theirs.
- They have no control over when they will be required to perform.
- They cannot, presumably, request a second chance to perform better what they do poorly on first effort.
- They cannot escape.

This is a GREAT list of high-stressor situation characteristics. So, in that setting, expect a lot of catecholamine to be floating through those little brains. Catecholamine narrows perceptual focus; it makes recall difficult; it makes anything difficult other than deciding whether to fight or flee.

If you happen to be a teacher of little kids, you could certainly help them get their physical stress responses well enough in hand to get through reading group. And if you're not a teacher of little kids, read the next several paragraphs anyway – what you'll read applies in principle to human beings of any age, including you and me.

Kiddie QR

While I was still administrating and teaching in the University of North Carolina system, I was asked to conduct stress-shaping classes for the children of undergraduate and graduate students.

Usually, we'd group the kids by two-year grade levels (e.g., first- and second-graders; third- and fourth-graders), and we'd limit enrollment in a particular class to about the size of the Bluebirds – six or seven kids. The "course" consisted of three weekly, 45-minute sessions.

The kids and I would usually spend the first session talking about "what worries you most" at school. These youngsters would describe the staggering pressures of daily school-world survival: avoiding the bullies; finding the right bus; remembering in which pocket (if any) the lunch money resides; finding the math homework; avoiding the bullies; remembering the instructions; staying awake; eating the canned pears; asking to go to the bathroom; avoiding the bullies; finding the pencil; finding the coat; finding the hat; finding the right bus; and, once more, avoiding the bullies. And, of course, getting through the daily ordeal of reading group.

Next, we'd turn to the related question: "How do you feel inside as you find yourself face to face, every day, with these things that worry you – the bullies, the elusive lunch money, the reading group?" They'd go through the litany: stomach in a knot most of the time, scared, mad, headache-y, quiet, loud, silly, tearful, "tearful in my throat," sad, really sad, throw-up sick, non-throw-up sick, dizzy, confused, lonesome for home.

Sobering as all this sounds, it made the kids feel better. It hadn't occurred to most of them that "everybody" felt the same way. They found this comforting.

I'd then send them off with the promise that in next week's session, I'd give them something they could use to help themselves get through it all. Most of them left smiling.

At the start of the second week's session, we'd review briefly. Then, I'd introduce Kiddie QR. ("QR" stands for "Quieting Reflex," which is the title of a book by Charles F. Stroebel, M.D., a psychiatrist in Hartford, CT.[1]) I taught those children just two of the components of QR; the results were *always* exciting.

First, I'd ask the kids to imagine they were sitting down for daily reading group. I'd ask them to picture in their minds the other members of the group, the teacher, and the classroom. Then I would introduce these two components of QR:

"Imagine," I'd say, "that you have holes in the bottoms of your feet." (Well, they liked this right away.) "And imagine," I'd continue, "that whenever you choose, you can breathe through those holes in the bottoms of your feet." (They'd laugh – this is great – we can breathe through holes in our feet.)

"The only other thing to remember is this," I'd add. "As you pull in a breath through those foot-holes, and as the imaginary breath comes up through your lower legs, then your upper legs, then your stomach, and finally up into your chest, *it relaxes all those muscles as it moves past them.* Then, as you send that breath back out the way it came in, it relaxes all the same muscles once more on its way out the foot-holes."

Well. What a thing. Holes in your feet, pulling a breath up through your legs and stomach into your chest, sending it back out the same way, and relaxing all the muscles "touched" by the breath, both coming and going.

The kids' responses ranged from wonder to relief:

"Hey, I can do *this*."

"Hey, this isn't even *hard*."

"Hey, nobody will even know I'm *doing* this."

1 *QR: The Quieting Reflex*, New York: Berkley Books, 1982.

Right. It's easy. It's "secret." And, because it's something you do in your mind, you can do it any time you want. Kids see right away, just as you do, what is happening. The mental trick of picturing the foot-holes, and of imagining the "breath" relaxing the muscles as it passes them, leads in fact to slower, more measured breathing and to less tension in the major muscle groups. The imagery guides the physiology.

Then, we'd practice. I'd have the children bring their reading books to the second and third sessions and we'd actually pretend to be the Bluebirds. They'd open their books, start breathing through the holes in their feet, and eventually they'd hear me say ... (pause) ... "Okay ... let's hear from YOU ... (pause) ... SANDRA!"

Upon hearing her name, Sandra would take one more foot-breath, compose herself, and begin to read.

Psychophysiology Revisited

Ridiculously simple, isn't it? But – you're asking – can anything this simple be ... ah ... valid? True? Correct? Consistent with research? In keeping with sound psychological and physiological principles?

In a word, yes. Of all the hundreds of discrete elements in the stress response – the neural signals, the releasing factors, the target organs, the hormones – you, I, and these kids have direct control over just two: respiration rate and depth, and striated muscle tension-relaxation.

If I asked you to, say, drop your systolic blood pressure by 10 or 15 points in the next 30 seconds, what would you do? In the first few seconds, you might just draw a blank. But then, if you're like most people, you might say something such as, "Well, maybe I'll just try to relax as much as I can ... maybe take some deep breaths."

Exactly. We don't have a way of issuing a direct order to the physiological complex that controls systolic blood pressure. We can't say to ourselves,

"All you smooth muscles in vascular networks: Relax!"

But we *can* say to ourselves: "Breathe slowly and deeply."

And we *can* say to ourselves: "Relax striated muscles." (The striated muscles, such as those in your legs, arms, and hands, respond to conscious direction – as distinct from "smooth muscles," which are found in internal organs, or "cardiac muscles," which constitute your heart.)

And here's the nice thing about all this. If you are breathing at something near your normal rate and depth, and if your major muscle groups are not tense, it is difficult for your stress response to feed upon itself and get out of hand. This is just plain, simple, correct psychophysiology.

That does not mean, of course, that correct breathing and relaxed major muscle groups combine to equal one completely unstressed human being. It means, rather, that correct breathing and relaxed major muscle groups combine to *retard the further development of the stress response.*

Have you ever watched basketball players on the foul line? Here's what you see, whether you're observing professional players, college players, high school players, or even younger ones: A foul is called, everything stops, the fouled player walks to the foul line for the free shot, the official hands the player the ball, and then ... a deep, slow breath, followed by efforts to relax the muscles, especially in the shooting arm ... and, finally, the shot.

Players learn early that if they can get the stress response under some control, they have a better chance of making the shot. And they do this even without a coach's explanation of the importance of respiration and striated muscle relaxation.

Why isn't this elementary psychophysiological insight routinely applied in classrooms? I assume because we associate this sort of stress shaping with athletic tasks, such as free-throw shooting, rather than with academic tasks, such as taking a timed arithmetic test in third grade, or writing an in-class American history essay in sixth grade, or taking the S.A.T.s in 11th grade. We do not even apply this rudimentary insight routinely to physical-performance academic tasks – such as delivering an oral book report to a roomful of not-necessarily-sympathetic peers.

And that's too bad. The stress response is preparing the mind to fight or flee just as thoroughly as it is preparing the body to fight or flee. And if the mind's task is to read in Bluebird group, what could be more beneficial than some means of *shaping* that stress response, of reducing catecholamine flow to the brain, and of *thereby permitting the best performance the student's ability and preparation will allow?*

Permit me one more point, related to kids (but indirectly related to us all). My youngest daughter participated in one of those stress-shaping classes that I taught back in North Carolina, when she was about 7 years old. She became a skilled QR-er. Several months later, she was given a speaking role in a school play that was to be performed, first, for the student body, and, second, for the parent body.

As opening night approached, I was callous enough to inquire of her one evening, "Erin, are you worried about delivering your lines in front of all those parents next Wednesday night?"

Hands on hips, she stared at me incredulously. "Don't you know?" she asked in a tone usually reserved for admonishing the cat, "I have **QR**!"

Your Physical Response

Erin's QR-related confidence as she approached her big performance carries with it an important message: HAVING A STRESS-SHAPING TECHNIQUE YOU CAN CALL ON AT ANY TIME TENDS TO ELEVATE BOTH SELF-CONFIDENCE AND SELF-ESTEEM. Thus, a physiological technique can have – and probably will have – positive psychological and emotional consequences.

I've provided this extended discussion of shaping kids' physical responses to illustrate how basic, how fundamental, and how easy this kind of stress shaping can be. The trick, as you noticed, is NOT in mastering a technique. A technique this simple is "mastered" almost as soon as it is described.

The trick is in *remembering to utilize the technique*. Will the kids remember to do QR? Yes, if you, as the teacher, do with QR what you do with other things that you want your students to know. That is, the students will remember to utilize QR if you give them practice, if you give them reinforcement, and if you "test" them on its usage. (And this is why, in those stress-shaping classes for children, we always prepared written explanations of the QR technique for the children's parents and for their teachers. We knew that without at-home and, we hoped, at-school reinforcement, the kids would probably "lose" the technique quickly.)

How about you? Do you need QR or some equivalent technique? And for what?

My answer to my own question is this – *the more stressful your life, the more you should be utilizing an in-action stress-shaping technique regularly.* Furthermore, the more stressful a given time period is for you, the more you should be regularly utilizing an in-action stress-shaping technique (recall here your Stressor Calendar). If your peak-stressor months are December, May, and November, you should have an in-action stress-shaping technique at your disposal especially for those annual peak periods.

For what situations would I recommend you employ an in-action stress-shaping technique? Every single one! Getting up and *thinking* about your school day, getting dressed, eating, getting in the car, driving in traffic (probably with your shoulders and your stomach in knots), walking into the school building, doing bus supervision, facing your home room ... the whole thing.

In other words, I think you ought to learn the technique I'm about to teach, use it frequently enough so that it becomes second nature, and make it become part of your everyday, every hour, every minute, "normal" functioning. It is really *not* something to call upon only during your toughest moments – such as in confrontations with students, with parents, or with administrators.

In a standard confrontation lasting, say, 60 seconds, I'd want you to be able to call upon your in-action stress-shaping technique two or three different times, so that you'd handle the confrontation better, and yet without triggering self-destructive internal responses. But that is *not* more important than being able to use the technique routinely, several dozen other times during a normal teaching day. It becomes, in other words, a way of "handling" your internal events, and a way that should, in my view, be regarded as indispensable for teachers and for anyone else who operates under continual stress.

By learning and becoming truly comfortable with such a technique, you give yourself the following benefits:

- lower levels of stress-related hormonal (and other) activity, including catecholamine and corticosteroid;
- a lower baseline of stress activity as each day wears on, thereby giving you more reserves with which to "immerse" yourself in *high-energy teaching;*
- because of that lower baseline of stress activity throughout the day, a better chance of being the person you'd like to be when you get home to your family, or your roommate(s), or your solitary evening activities and responsibilities;
- more mental clarity to bring to bear on your most challenging discussions and in your most difficult confrontations (and, thus, a better chance of saying "the right thing" in the midst of emotion-laden exchanges);
- a "presence" which may or may not have been otherwise obvious in your interactions with students, parents, and others.

Counting Down

At the start of Chapter 7 ("Psychophysiology 101: Teaching from the Inside Out"), I described the "performance exams" I used to give to college students. When I completed that description, I wrote:

The students had learned to shape stress under very difficult – albeit contrived – circumstances. And that was the point. Anybody can shape stress (with just a little instruction) while lying peacefully alone in bed. But who cares?

> *The issue is: Can you shape your stress profile and yet remain thoroughly immersed – in one of the most stressful occupations yet invented? Can you teach and shape your stress profile at the same time? If you want to maintain your energy levels and high performance, you'll have to.*

If you work with your Stressor Calendar (Chapter 8), you can immediately start to reshape your stress**or** profile. If you start to engage in

Ritual Reflection (Chapter 9), you can immediately start to reshape your internal reactions to stress.

Now, if you put into practice the in-action stress-shaping technique I'm about to teach called Counting Down, you can do what those college students learned to do, year after year: remain immersed in the minute-to-minute whirlwind of life while maintaining moderate, productive, non-damaging levels of internal endocrine-and-neural activity.

Let me be clear on this. This is not the stuff of exotic, enigmatic, inscrutable, self-hypnotic, semi-magical trance states. *Counting Down is exactly like Kiddie QR except in the imagery it employs to get its stress-shaping, stress-braking effects. By that I mean that it is simple; it requires no "time-out"; it is not self-hypnotic; and it* **is** *physiologically sound. And, like Kiddie QR, human beings will actually do it willingly.*[2]

Counting Down has a practice version and an in-action version. Don't confuse the two. The *practice* version, if you were to use it publicly, would get you hooted out of your classroom for conspicuous weirdness. The *in-action* version, similar to Kiddie QR, is not visible to anyone and is thus, as the kids used to say about QR, a "secret weapon."

Instructions for both the practice and the in-action versions of Counting Down are displayed on the next two pages.

---

2 Note: I should also make clear that Dr. Stroebel's procedure, QR, is an adult technique. Its modification for children is called Kiddie QR. If you read Dr. Stroebel's book, previously cited in this chapter, you will read a perspective very much like the one presented here. I personally like Counting Down for adults and QR for kids, but QR can have applications for all ages, not just children.

Counting Down: The Private, Practice Version

Carve out 10 minutes to do this:

1. Go into a private room. Close the door. Close your eyes.
2. Take a couple of minutes to think about your stressors – your background and foreground worries of the day. Get as tense as you'd like.
3. Making sure nobody is looking (this is the weird part), crank up the muscle tension in your entire musculo-skeletal system: clench your hands into fists; tighten your biceps; curl your toes; tense the muscles in your lower and upper legs, your abdomen, your chest, your shoulders, and, without fail, your face! That means your face will turn into one big, ugly wrinkle. Do it anyway. Nobody's looking.
4. Hold that whole-body tension for about 10 seconds.
5. At that point, mentally divide your body into three parts:

   Part Three: head, neck, shoulders, arms.

   Part Two: torso.

   Part One: legs.

   Say to yourself the number "Three," and immediately relax the muscles in your head, neck, shoulders, and arms. Maintain the tension in Parts Two and One.
6. Think how that feels – all that relaxation in Part Three.
7. After about 10 seconds of that, say to yourself the number "Two," and immediately relax the muscles in your torso – chest and abdomen – AND *concentrate on returning to a slow, relaxed, normal pattern of breathing.*
8. Think how that feels – all that relaxation in Parts Three and Two.
9. After about 10 seconds of that, say to yourself the number "One," and immediately relax the muscles in your legs.
10. Think how that feels – all that relaxation in your whole musculo-skeletal system, and that comfortable, slow, regular breathing.

11. Without the slightest change in your physiology, let your mind go to your tension points and mentally confirm the relaxation you have ordered: your forehead, your jaw (Can you slip your tongue between your upper and lower teeth? Why not?), your shoulders (Can you drop them at all? Why?), your abdomen (Is your stomach moving in and out as you breathe? It should be).

12. *Commit this feeling to memory: relaxed, breathing normally, and yet fully alert.* Alert and relaxed ARE compatible states!

Now, repeat this process, steps #3-12, several more times, going more rapidly on each series. On the final run-through, say the "Three-Two-One" to yourself as rapidly as you can say the numbers. At that speed, there is no sense of differentiating among the three "Parts" of your body; there is only the mental/physical wave-like sensation of near-instant relaxation and return to normal breathing.

Before you sign off on your practice session, do this without fail: In this state of thorough relaxation accompanied by slow, regular breathing, gradually let your mind return to #2 – thinking about your stress<u>ors</u> – for a couple of minutes. Then say "Three-Two-One" quickly to yourself, and thereby recapture your relaxation and your slow breathing. Switch back and forth several times, *without any purposeful tensing*, from stressor-thinking to Counting Down and back again. End your Counting Down practice session with one more Count Down and a pleasant, self-congratulatory message to yourself.

The caveats:

1. Whole-body tensing will drive up your blood pressure; if you have hypertension or other cardiovascular weaknesses, make the whole-body tensing no more than very slight muscular contractions in your extremities; leave the torso out of the tensing so that you can maintain normal breathing.

2. Understand that you cannot maintain normal breathing, but that you should not purposely hold your breath during the tensing portion. Breathe as well as you can with abdomen and chest muscles held tense.

3. Question: "You said to close my eyes. How do I know when I've

practiced for 10 minutes?" Answer: "Look at your watch." This is not self-hypnosis; this is not a trance. **It is skill development**.

4. Question: "Won't people notice when I scrunch up my face in public?" Answer: "Yes. I warned you not to do the practice version of Counting Down in public. That will not, let's say, advance your career."

Counting Down: The In-Action Version

The paragraph on the previous page which starts with the words, "Before you sign off ... do this without fail," actually describes the in-action version of Counting Down. You know when you are facing stressors. You face them several times an hour at school. When you do, say to yourself (in the "back of your mind"), "Three-Two-One." Do no purposeful tensing.

That cue, invoked in a split second *while* you continue to engage your stressor, calls into play these two braking forces: less tension in the major muscle groups; and slower, deeper respiration. The effects are immediate and profound.

Sample sequence: (1) You sense two of your seventh-grade boys starting to act like seventh-grade boys; (2) as you walk toward them, you Count Down, putting the brakes on your network of fluid and electrical stress-and-rage generators; (3) the verbal interaction does not go well, but when the boys are speaking to you, you Count Down, each time, thereby keeping your brain relatively catecholamine-free and able to form the "right" thoughts. The confrontation ends unsatisfactorily. Nevertheless, you have been assertive; you have meted out instructions and/or punishment of some sort; and you have neither demeaned nor alienated these two characters. You have not damaged yourself internally, or damaged your ability to shape the attitudes of these two students. *In the real world of classrooms, this is very good work indeed.*

How often should you do the practice version of Counting Down? Some regular users of in-action Counting Down have only practiced once in their entire lives, and that was when I talked them through the practice version in class or in a workshop. They walked out the door at the end of the workshop and started using the technique, in-action, and never needed to practice again.

That's the best answer I can give. There are people who practice once a week or more. There are others who never practice. Use of Counting Down several times a day, in the midst of other activities, is practice.

You get better at in-action Counting Down by doing in-action Counting Down. Using the **practice** version a lot probably constitutes what I call a "time-out" stress-shaping technique, similar to some forms of meditation or progressive relaxation, and certainly of value in itself. (In fact, Counting Down's originators, St. Lawrence University professors Theodore Renick and Hugh Gunnison, designed the technique for that kind of use.[3] I changed my then-colleagues' time-out technique to an in-action procedure.)

High-Energy or Comatose?

Back in the late '70s, when the United States hosted the Winter Olympic Games, I gave a one-day workshop on renewal/performance/stress for the Winter Olympic Organizing Committee in Lake Placid, New York. Never had I before, nor have I since, worked with a group that seemed to be running so fast to keep from falling behind. About 50 people sat on the edge of their seats throughout, in a supercharged, let-me-get-back-to-the-telephone atmosphere. They weren't discourteous. They just wanted to "get" everything I had to offer in, say, 30 minutes, rather than six hours.

Under those circumstances, I knew that Counting Down was the *only* thing that could help them at all. They weren't about to reshape their stressor calendars; they weren't going to do an hour per month of Ritual Reflection; they certainly weren't going to do those techniques which require even more time-out – techniques such as meditation or progressive relaxation – than the techniques I teach and advocate. It was Counting Down or nothing.

So, I really worked, both at selling them on the concept and at teach-

3 Gunnison, H., "Fantasy Relaxation Technique," *Personnel and Guidance Journal,* 55:299-300, 1976.

ing the technique. When I finished with both, I felt pleased. They seemed excited, enthusiastic, and grateful. I was especially pleased at the kinds of questions I got from the group. They were good questions, designed to deepen their understanding of the physiology involved, or to help refine their in-action (simulated) skills. We practiced the practice version repeatedly, and we practiced the in-action version in numerous simulations, many of which involved telephone situations that they faced every day.

Then came the comment that sent me mentally back to the drawing board. A man looked up from his note pad (which no doubt is where his mind had been for some time), sighed audibly and impatiently, and made this statement. "This is pretty interesting, I guess, for people who don't have much to do. But I'm going a hundred miles an hour from 3 a.m. when my first European phone calls come in, until 11 p.m., when my last Japanese and Australian phone calls come in. I can't go around Counting Down – *in some kind of a coma* – 20 hours every day. I have to be alert all the time to do my job. You just don't understand what it's like here."

In my best instructional manner, I tried to use his colossal misunderstanding of everything I'd been teaching for the previous two hours to re-teach Counting Down's basic premises. Like you, I assumed that if one person had missed it by that much, then so, probably, had at least a few others. So, I hit the high points once more:

- Counting Down takes no "time out."
- Counting Down allows you to remain mentally "in gear" with your stressors, regardless of how frequently you employ the technique in a given day. Some people use Counting Down routinely more than a hundred times a day.
- Counting Down becomes, if you choose, your basic way of "handling" minute-to-minute stressors physiologically, *so that you* ***can*** *function as well as possible mentally* – clear, sharp, alert, focused.

In fact, I explained, when I give instruction in public speaking, I insist that the students pencil onto their note cards the letters "CD" at numerous points to remind themselves that an important part of delivering an oral presentation is this kind of in-action stress shaping. Listeners tend to interpret an apparently controlled physiological state as "poise" in their own minds. Student public speakers who learn to Count Down during their presentations get comments from other audiences such as, "You seemed upbeat and calm at the same time. How'd you do that?"

If follow-up surveys have made anything clear over the years, it is this. People will do Counting Down when they won't do anything else in the whole field of stress shaping. Americans, suffering from what cardiologists Meyer Friedman and Ray Rosenman first called "the hurry sickness,"[4] are just too rushed to **stop** and take care of their own stress levels. Counting Down is designed to be done on the run. It's perfect.

Are you starting to see where this book's title comes from? High-Energy Teaching is the most descriptive phrase I can devise for the teacher who is striving to develop her or his technical excellence AND who is formulating a self-renewal system built on continual recommitment to First Purposes. Chapters 8, 9, and 10's stress-shaping tools –

- environmental (the Stressor Calendar),
- psychological/emotional (Ritual Reflection), and
- in-action physiological (Counting Down or QR)

– are designed to link with your technical-excellence goals, whatever those may be, to keep you emotionally grounded in your First Purposes, and psychophysiologically grounded in high performance.

Exchange ideas with your peers and with Walker Buckalew about in-action stress shaping – call the **Teachers In Touch** ***newsletter.***

Call 1-800-955-4944.

4 Friedman, M., & Rosenman, R., *Type A Behavior and Your Heart*, New York: Fawcett Crest, 1974.

Chapter 11

Shaping the Core System: CV Renewal (the Ultimate Stress Shaper)

Four nights a week, after she puts her children to bed, a school administrator I know does an unusual thing. She goes into her den and takes a seat in a special chair.

This chair is positioned under a reading light, in front of the television, next to the phone. Of the three activities implied, she more often than not chooses a telephone conversation.

For 30 to 40 minutes, she talks on the phone with one or more of her friends. She's been doing this now for four years. She enjoys it, and plans to continue with this habit for the rest of her life. When her kids grow up, she'll be free to alter the time schedule if she likes. And when she retires – far into the future – she'll be even more able to schedule these chats to her convenience.

What's special about the chair she uses four nights a week? It is a piece of equipment that we commonly refer to, I'm sorry to say, as an exercise bicycle. If I could get every adult in America to call those exercise bicycles "The Special Telephone Chair," or "The Special Reading Chair," or "The Special Television Chair," or, in the case of teachers, "The Special Renewal Chair," maybe those misused, misunderstood pieces of equipment wouldn't find themselves in practically every garage sale I've ever seen. They are potentially one of the cheapest, most convenient life-savers and career-savers around. But hardly anybody thinks of them that way.

Another school administrator I know keeps a standing rendezvous with two of her friends every morning at 5:30. They meet, walk together through their neighborhood for 30 minutes, and return home. This school administrator then gets her kids out the door, gets dressed, and heads for school. She's been doing this for five years now.

When I was younger and stupider, I'd go out on the roads and run – hard and fast – every day, for miles. One evening, near the end of what was probably my daily 10-mile run, I found myself swiftly overtaking another runner, the wife of a good friend.

I remember thinking to myself how interesting it was that anyone could actually run as slowly as she was running. In fact, the thought occurred to me fleetingly that, if a person ran that slowly, she or he might enjoy it a little. (I *said* I was stupid.) She was "running" slower than most people walk. And I mean that literally.

Then, to my further astonishment, just as I was drawing close enough to say hello to her, she stopped, still unaware of my presence, bent over, and PICKED A FLOWER!

"Hi Kris," I said, as I flew by.

"Hi ... ," I heard faintly from behind me, in the rapidly increasing distance.

The Ultimate Stress Shaper

The "Core System" to which this chapter's title refers is your cardiovascular system. I call it the "core" because it is in that system that so many of the most powerful performance/health/stress forces play themselves out. And as you would guess, measurements related to that system are often of the most interest to those who attend to the performance/health/stress equation.

The "Ultimate Stress Shaper" is any activity, such as the ones I just depicted to start this chapter, that has a direct, positive impact on the cardiovascular system. I'll refer to this kind of activity as "Cardiovascular (CV) Renewal."

Because, by definition, stress is a physiological – not psychological – phenomenon, the cardiovascular system's excellence or mediocrity has a great deal to do with how well you handle the stressors you face. The cardiovascular system reacts instantly and powerfully to your stressors, as you've sensed from the days in your own childhood when you were old enough to understand the meaning of the words, "My heart was pounding so hard I thought it would come through my chest."

Engaging in CV Renewal while sitting in a Special Renewal Chair, while walking with a couple of friends at 5:30 a.m., or while running slower than most people can walk, are all superb examples of the Ultimate Stress Shaper in action.

Superficially speaking, your physiology runs like an automobile engine. That is, it accelerates or decelerates in response to commands from its brain. Its performance is a function of what its brain asks it to do, *and* of its "conditioning." If the engine is not cared for regularly, it will eventually struggle when you place heavy demands upon it. In fact, if unattended, it will eventually struggle even when you place *ordinary* demands upon it.

Physiologically, human beings are simply not designed to function in the way we assume they are. In the industrialized nations of the world, most of us do the equivalent of leaving our engines unattended, day after day, month after month, year after year, decade after decade.

We *feel* extremely busy. And we are. We fail to realize, in our extreme busy-ness, that we mostly sit (even while going somewhere), stand, or walk very short distances (from the car to the classroom; from the front of the classroom to the back; from the classroom to the lunchroom).

Teachers "do not have time" to attend to their engines, either the ones in their automobiles or the metaphorical one that I'm really talking about here. It can't be done. You cannot teach school, "do the family," fulfill your neighborhood, community, social, and other responsibilities, and attend to your engine. Impossible. Or so most of us think.

So it is that teachers' baseline stress levels run as high as they do. It is not just that teachers' stress<u>ors</u> are extraordinarily high, although, as I've discussed, they certainly are. It is also that most teachers' engines (like those of most other Americans) are in mediocre condition, thereby exacerbating what is already a serious problem.

To extend the metaphor just a little further – teachers operate with engines that are poorly conditioned, and try to do so despite the fact that, because they are teachers, they drive only up steep hills (stressors). Never downhill. Never even flat. Just up.

The three women I described in starting this chapter have figured out ways to condition their engines so that they can run uphill continually, yet strongly. Each one has analyzed the demands on her time, and has constructed an approach that fits her needs and her schedule.

CV Renewal

Notice I'm not using the word "exercise." Most people, hearing that word, picture something I don't mean. I mean a person sitting in a Special Renewal Chair four nights a week after the kids are in bed, talking on the phone with friends. I mean a person meeting friends in the early morning to walk and talk before the day starts. I mean a person jogging slower than you can walk, looking at birds and trees, and stopping to pick flowers.

As your engine becomes better conditioned by virtue of your engaging in some regular activity, everything in your physiology which you'd wish to run lower or slower (e.g., LDL cholesterol, or diastolic blood pressure, or resting heart rate, or peaking heart rate under stress – see page 142 for definitions) tends to run, in fact, lower or slower. And everything you'd wish to run higher or faster (e.g., HDL cholesterol, or basal metabolism, or time of recovery to baseline pulse after stress peaks – see page 142 for definitions) tends to run, in fact, higher or faster.

Think about what engaging in regular CV Renewal does for you. It means that, even in your highest-stressor month (December, in our ongoing example from Chapter 5), your baseline physiological stress levels – and all those related renewal/performance/health numbers that go with those levels – are running much closer to the ideal than they otherwise would be. It means that, no matter what the stressor, or how severe the stressor, or of what duration the stressor, your physiology departs a shorter distance from its CV-Renewal-enhanced baseline, and returns to that CV-Renewal-enhanced baseline much more quickly.

CV Renewal – The Ultimate Stress Shaper – is "ultimate" for the following reasons. Look at each of these carefully.

With regular usage:

- your performance/health/stress baseline is enhanced;
- in the face of daily stressors, your departure from your enhanced baseline is smaller;
- in the face of daily stressors, your return to your enhanced baseline is much quicker;
- your HDL cholesterol can be expected to climb (an *extremely* important heart-disease-related variable – the higher the better);
- your diastolic blood pressure can be expected to drop, if it was elevated to begin with (a change that is arguably as important as is the just-mentioned change in HDL cholesterol levels);
- your resting heart rate will drop, indicating its greater efficiency in getting oxygen and nutrients to your cells;
- your metabolic rate will climb, indicating a more rapid burning of calories, *even while you are at rest* (that is, even while you are not engaging in CV Renewal);
- your body-fat percentage will decline (understand that this decrease in percent body fat does not necessarily translate into *weight* loss – muscle cells are much more dense than fat cells, and so your "shape" may change without your weight being reduced);
- your cardiopulmonary/cardiovascular system's ability to "load" oxygen and nutrients into your bloodstream, and to deliver the oxygen and nutrients to every cell in your body – your energy transport system – becomes increasingly efficient, thus allowing you to have steadily improving levels of what we (non-technically) refer to as "stamina."

What should my numbers be?

"Good" numbers vary. The ones following will give you a feel for what your own target values might be. Consider these to be approximations (as, in fact, are most of the measurements themselves).

- **High-density lipids (HDL cholesterol)** Women – 55 mg/dl or higher.
  Men – 43 mg/dl or higher.
  Pre-menopausal women have a head start on men, thanks apparently to the effects of estrogen. After menopause, women tend to lose this advantage, and synthetic estrogen may or may not restore the advantage.
  Measurement: blood test. *Ask* when your blood is drawn that HDL be included. Otherwise, only your total cholesterol may be reported. See my comments below on total cholesterol.

- **Low-density lipids (LDL cholesterol)** 130 mg/dl or lower.
  Some authorities will suggest that this number changes with age. The average does go up with age. That does not imply that your LDL **should** increase with age.
  Measurement: blood test. *Ask* for the LDL value when your blood is drawn.

- **Total cholesterol** A worthless number.
  Although "Get your total cholesterol under 200" is a common refrain, it is a misleading message. Why add a "good" number, HDL, to a "bad" number, LDL, and attend to the total as if it were meaningful? If your total cholesterol were, in fact, 200, but composed of an HDL level of 65, an LDL level of 125, and a Very Low-Density Lipid (VLDL) level of 10, you should be delighted. But if your total were still 200, and composed of HDL at 35, LDL at 155, and VLDL at 10, you should be concerned.

- **Diastolic blood pressure** 80 mm/Hg or under.
  This is the lower number when your result is

	reported to you. It is the pressure within your arteries between "blood blobs," as your heart rhythmically pushes blood through your cardiovascular system. **Measurement**: blood pressure cuff. Can be done with acceptable accuracy at home, using equipment purchased in drug stores.
• **Systolic blood pressure**	120 mm/Hg or under. This is the upper number when your result is reported to you. It is the pressure within your arteries as the "blood blob" passes through them, distending them fully. **Measurement:** see diastolic, above.
• **Resting heart rate**	65 bpm or lower. Your resting pulse is a good indicator of your cardiovascular system's conditioning. In a well-conditioned system, your heart does not need to beat very often when it is at rest. The CV system is a demand system. Your heart will, at rest, beat as seldom as it can and still pump oxygen and nutrients to your cells. **Measurement**: place your finger lightly on your wrist or on one of your interior carotid arteries in your neck; count for 60 seconds.
• **Percent body fat**	Women – 20% or less. Men – 15% or less. This is the percent of your total weight which is composed of fat cells. It is a more useful statement about your body composition than is weight. Women's higher target level represents recognition of the inherent fattiness in child-nurturing organs. **Measurement:** can be measured approximately with a skinfold caliper instrument, using conversion tables; can be measured *accurately* by an underwater weighing device.

Collectively, these changes in your physiology are core elements in the "**high-energy**" approach to **teaching**. Without an "engine" that is well-conditioned, you place yourself at a disadvantage in your efforts to be continually self-renewing. You will be unlikely to have the stamina needed to remain continually "immersed" with your students, and you will be unlikely to have the sustained vigor needed to remain continually excited about your career and its ongoing development.

CV Renewal: the Process

So, what must teachers do to reap the benefits just listed?

Do your own version of the CV Renewal process exemplified by the women I've described. There is the Renewal Chair (or other kinds of equipment), the morning walk, the unbelievably slow jog. There is, in short, any activity that causes your cardiovascular system to work a little harder than usual for 20 minutes or more each time, and in which you engage at least three times a week.

That's it. It's as simple – and as impossible – as that. Simple, because it can just mean, literally, walking around. Impossible, because you have no time to do it.

That's why I started the chapter with those three vignettes. Those are real human beings, doing the right thing. They don't have any time either. They're not particularly athletic (they tell me). They're just determined to gain and retain the benefits – professional and personal – which go hand in hand with engaging in the Ultimate Stress Shaper. They know it's not convenient, but they know, too, that there is no substitute for it.

If you are part of a family, as most of you are, you may or may not have to ask the family to help you in your efforts. The school administrator who "rides" her Special Renewal Chair after putting the kids to bed, Monday through Thursday nights, hasn't had to ask for adjustments by her family members. The school administrator who walks with her two friends at 5:30 every morning, on the other hand, has had to enlist the cooperation of her husband and her kids – they all get up and prepare for the day before she completes her walk.

Think about the likelihood that you will encounter opposition within your own family and/or within your own faculty. People of good will who love you may, nonetheless, not be happy that you intend to introduce changes of any sort into the conduct of your life – especially if it requires any adjustments on their parts. And maybe even if it does *not* require adjustments on their parts. They may, frankly, feel a little jealous of your determination. A little envious. A little resentful. And so they may try to subvert your efforts, either subconsciously or consciously, by subtle means or by overt means.

Just be prepared for it. Expect it. Think what you'll do with it.

CV Renewal: How Do I Know I'm Doing This Right?

You know you're doing CV Renewal right if:

- you don't perspire while you're doing it (unless it's because the room is hot);
- you're never out of breath while you're doing it;
- you're never tired at the end of it;
- you're never sore the next day;
- you never miss more than three consecutive days of doing it unless you're sick.

Be clear on this: Your commitment is NOT to doing 20 minutes or more of CV Renewal activity, three or more times a week. That is the **goal**. Your commitment is to engage in some gentle, large-muscle activity on a regular, scheduled basis, and to *observe the guidelines I just wrote*: never sweating (except from heat), never breathless, never tired, never sore, never missing more than three consecutive days (except for sickness). THAT is the commitment. Given those guidelines, you may be engaged in CV Renewal for six **months** before you reach the point at which you can comfortably do 20 continuous minutes of your Renewal activity, and do it three times a week. (But bear this in mind. If you cannot, after six **weeks**, sustain your CV Renewal activity for 20 minutes, you're probably working at much too high an intensity level. Slow down. You have the WRONG IDEA! You're still thinking in "exercise" terms. This is CV Renewal! It is not like anything else you've ever done.)

Although it must sound to you as if I'm kidding, I'm really not. The only way to do CV Renewal "wrong" is to do it too hard, too fast, too intensely. Do this at a level that leads you not to hate it, not to be out of breath while you're doing it or after you finish, not to be sore the next day. You should be able to talk throughout. You should, if you're using a Special Renewal Chair for your CV Renewal, also be able to read, to watch television, possibly even to write.

How can something so gentle really deserve such a label as I've given it – the Ultimate Stress Shaper? It is the *regularity* of the procedure that produces the renewal effects. Not the intensity (how fast and how hard). It is the duration (20 minutes-plus), and the frequency (three times-plus per week) that produce the CV Renewal effects. When your physiology finally gets the message that it will actually be required to **do** something on a regular basis, it will change. Count on it.

And you will then have converted your mediocre, inefficient cardiovascular system (and related systems) into a physical vehicle capable of sustaining your overall renewal program – your *high-energy* teaching.

But Wait! I'm an Athlete!

Oh. You're an athlete?

I'm glad you're an athlete. But I have to tell you, the ability and willingness of athletes to comply with a CV Renewal program is poor, in comparison to less athletic individuals.

I have no trouble recalling my first five-mile run, although it was many years ago. I told my St. Lawrence University faculty colleagues in our noon-hour basketball group that I was going to take three months "off" from basketball, so that I could prepare to run in the Canadian National Capital Marathon in Ottawa.

Marathons are 26.2 miles in length. I reasoned, idiotically, that the way to prepare for that was to start at about five miles, run that far or longer every day for three months, and then go do the race.

So, one February noon-hour in upstate New York, I took to the roads. Settling into a pace just slightly slower than a basketball fast break,

I darted off into the wintry countryside. I found this to be enormously hard work physically. But what struck me hardest was the *mental* difficulty of this activity.

Where was the ball? The goal? The opponents? My teammates? The sidelines? The officials? The fans? And, above all, WHAT WAS THE SCORE?

I had nothing to think about. Except how very uncomfortable this solitary, unrewarding activity seemed to be. "Why," I asked myself every few steps, "would anyone possibly choose to do this?"

And that's why athletes so often fail to comply with a CV Renewal regimen. It's not sports.

Of course, what I was doing on that frigid February day was not CV Renewal, either. That was anything but a gentle, careful, take-good-care-of-yourself, slower-than-you-can-walk "jog." It was a self-destructive semi-sprint.

And that points up the fact that athletes have two problems here: first, what do you do in your mind; and second, how can you do any physical activity at a level of intensity so ridiculously far below your capacity?

There is no easy answer to the first question. The trick is to stop thinking of CV Renewal activities as sport. That's hard to do.

But you must. Once you think of it as CV Renewal – an activity like no other activity – you have a chance at a psychological breakthrough for yourself. You have a chance to do what my exemplar women in this chapter have learned to do with their minds: focus on a conversation with friends, take thoughtful note of the scenery around you on an outdoor walk, become lost in a book or newspaper, concentrate on the news on TV, immerse yourself in problem-solving or planning scenarios.

When you think of it that way, a light bulb may go on in your sports-drenched mind. What an opportunity! You can actually engage in CV Renewal and, at the same time, accomplish any number of other interesting, useful, and/or emotionally renewing things. This can be a great thing for you.

As for the second question – how can you make yourself engage in physical activity at a level so far below your capacity – do some reading on this topic. Look at the data produced, for example, by Dr. Kenneth Cooper's clinic in Dallas.[1] There, the preeminent studies of their kind have established – incontrovertibly, in my opinion – that remarkably low-intensity activity has profound cardiovascular (and overall physiological health) benefits for those who engage in it regularly. Satisfy yourself that the evidence is there. And then make your commitment.

But, athletes persist, does CV Renewal activity **have** to be so gentle that you don't even *perspire*? No. Perspire if you must. But if you're working at an intensity level that does not allow you to have a conversation with a friend who is walking next to you, or with a family member reclining in the chair next to your Special Renewal Chair – you're not doing what I'm talking to you about in this chapter. You'll have to call it something else. Like exercise.

"Type B" Activity

We were able to put together some interesting, descriptive research projects on the University of North Carolina's Asheville campus in the early 1980s. We examined the idea that, for "Type A" people especially, the attitude CV Renewers brought to their activity might speed up or slow down the physiological changes normally to be expected as a result of that activity.

You've read about Type A/Type B "personalities." And you'll remember that, earlier, I mentioned Dr. Meyer Friedman and Dr. Ray Rosenman (authors of the 1974 classic, *Type A Behavior and Your Heart*).

Picture yourself listening to an interviewer in one approach to Type A/Type B evaluation. You want to know if you're Type A (typically described as hard-driving, goal-oriented victims of the "hurry sickness") or Type B (the reverse). You're being videotaped as you go through the interview.

The interviewer speaks extraordinarily slowly and carefully even

---

[1] For more information, contact The Cooper Institute for Aerobic Research, 12330 Preston, Dallas, TX 75230.

when not hesitating between words. Let this imaginary interviewer's words play through your mind slowly, as if this interviewer were speaking directly to you. React the way you really might:

"So ... you find ... ah ... that ... ah ... when you go to work on Monday ... Tuesday ... ah ... um ... Wednesday ... Thursday, and ... ah ... ah ... ah ... ummm ... Friday ... you tend to ... ah ... give some thought to ... ah ... whether or not ... ah ... ah ... you are in the ... ah ... ah ... profession, for reasons somewhat different from ... ah ... um ... those with which you ... ah ... ah ... entered the ... ah ... ah ... ah ... profession ... back in ... ah ... in ... ah ... ah ... ah ... ."

There.

What would the videotape of your response show? Would it show a relaxed listener, a trifle bemused at the interviewer's halting, absent-minded, lethargic delivery? Or would it show an increasingly tense listener, finishing some phrases for the interviewer, moving hands and feet and facial muscles in impatience? Would you, the listener, be tightening your stomach muscles involuntarily, clenching your teeth in frustration, raging internally at this infuriating speech pattern?

In our UNCA studies, we developed short paper-and-pencil questionnaires to give us a feel for this complicated issue of where a given individual might fall on the Type A/Type B continuum, both in daily, moment-to-moment activities, and *during CV Renewal activity*. Then we took blood samples to determine HDL cholesterol levels for each individual.

Our findings are summarized by the figure on the following page.

The vertical axis on the "CV Renewal and HDL cholesterol" figure depicts measured levels of high-density lipids (HDL cholesterol), with the scale inverted to show highest levels at the bottom and lowest levels at the top (since, with HDL, the more, the better). The horizontal axis shows number of minutes engaged per week in CV Renewal activity.

The message of the figure is straightforward. Those Type A individuals whose attitudes toward their CV Renewal activity were non-competitive, low-key, and relaxed showed HDL levels associated with very low heart disease risk even with small time commitments each week. Those Type A individuals whose attitudes toward their CV Renewal activity were

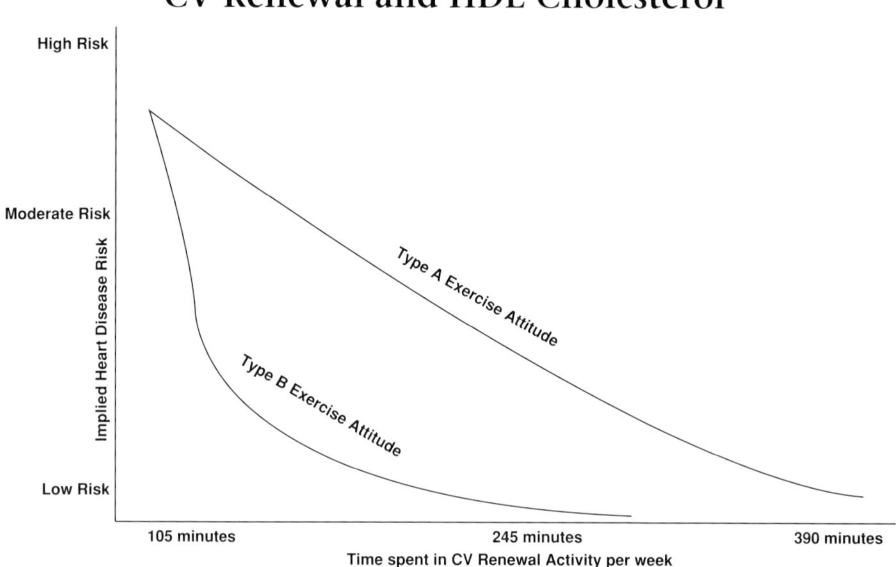

Type A individuals who maintain their competitive, hurried, attitudes while engaged in CV Renewal Activity reduce implied heart disease risks as their aerobic time commitment grows, but the improvement is much less dramatic than that found in Type A individuals who become Type B while engaging in CV Renewal activity – non-competitive, less hurried, more cheerful.

"Type A" – who, in the parlance of *High-Energy Teaching*, were "exercising" hard and fast – showed HDL levels that were as outstanding as those of their lower-key, CV Renewal counterparts *only when they reached extremely high levels of time committed to the activity each week.*

As with a good deal of the research in this complex area of Type A/ Type B "personalities," our UNCA findings cannot prove that, if you switch your CV Renewal attitude from a Type A approach to the one I recommend throughout this chapter, your HDL levels will improve more dramatically. But the findings do *imply* that this would happen.

And the findings are certainly compatible with everything I know about the relationships between CV Renewal attitudes, on the one hand (low-key, relaxed, and *non-competitive **during** the activity*), and "exercise attitudes," on the other (keyed-up, hard-driving, and competitive during the activity).

Combinations and Implications

Think now of your Stressor Calendar. How about those top stressor months of yours (December, May, and November in Chapter 5's examples)? Is your CV Renewal activity something to retain, on schedule, no matter what your Stressor Calendar looks like? Or is it something to give up or reduce under maximum-stressor conditions?

My answer is that this should depend upon the CV Renewal activity (or activities) you settle on. If you decide on a CV Renewal activity that permits only limited concurrent activity – like slower-than-you-can-walk jogging, or use of a machine (like, maybe, a stair climber) which makes it hard to read during the activity – I'd suggest that you reduce the frequency of your CV Renewal habit. Not the duration. The frequency.

Instead of three weekly sessions of 20 minutes each, do two. Or alter the schedule to a one-day-in-four routine (e.g., Monday, Friday, Tuesday, Saturday). Hang onto the 20 minutes-per-session.

Or, alternatively, switch your CV Renewal activity to one that *does* permit *concurrent activities of the sort which help you keep up with your stressors*. The Special Renewal Chair (exercise bicycle) allows reading or even writing, the latter with some difficulty. The Special Renewal Treadmill (with music stand or other creative book-holding device) allows reading, provided you are walking and not jogging. The more weight you put on your hands (which will be grasping the machine's railings), the smoother your treadmill walking will become. The Special Renewal Lounge Chair (recumbent exercise bicycle) allows almost any intellectual activity imaginable. Hands are completely free; torso and head are stable.

Real life is filled with trade-offs. Decide what yours need to be. If, in your highest-stressor periods, you need to reduce the frequency of your CV Renewal activity, just do that and don't worry about it. Yes, you will lose some of your CV conditioning. And you'll need to start back slowly. (Your muscles will remind you of that, I assure you.) But you're smart enough to prioritize, to plan, and to implement your plan.

Be committed to your CV Renewal program, but do not become obsessed with it. You're working on your "spirit of renewal," your commitment to First Purposes, your excitement about your career, and your stamina in pursuing this level of commitment.

Your CV Renewal activity *must serve that goal, not substitute for it.*

Final Notes

I've called CV Renewal the Ultimate Stress Shaper. It's also an Ultimate something else: It's the Ultimate Safety Net.

By that, I mean that it allows you to be flawed – to be human – in all your other performance/health/stress-shaping efforts, and still be "mostly okay," as your kids might say. It allows you to "forget" to do in-action stress shaping (Counting Down and/or QR), and still have the stamina to get through your worst day. It allows you to neglect your commitment to Ritual Renewal, and still be mentally "clear" enough to get through your worst week without losing direction. It allows you to fail to adjust your stressor calendar for your highest-stressor month, and still (maybe) not get sick during or after it. It is, in short, a great insurance policy.

And all that, I should add, is in *addition* to the value of CV Renewal in combating industrial societies' number one killer, coronary artery disease. The build-up of plaque in your coronary arteries (the ones that transport oxygen and nutrients to the heart itself, and which, therefore, lie embedded in the walls of the heart) is the result of how you eat and how you "exercise." Excess LDL cholesterol is part of the problem; insufficient HDL cholesterol is the other part of the problem. One adds to the plaque; the other counteracts the plaque. If excess LDL is present, while insufficient HDL is present, plaque collects in the coronary arteries, restricting blood flow until eventually there is a blockage.

This is a "heart attack." The result is the death of muscle cells in the vicinity of the blockage. If enough cells die, the heart stops. If the heart is able to continue to pump despite the death of a portion of its muscle cells, you become a heart-attack survivor.

We know that until the mid-'70s, heart-attack survivors were treated as invalids, forbidden by most physicians to be active for the rest of their lives. And we know that now the treatment for heart-attack recovery is exactly what you've just been reading: CV Renewal.

Medical research has found that if heart-attack survivors enter the kind of graduated, gentle approach to "exercise" that I've described throughout this chapter, remarkable things happen. The cardiovascular system *grows new capillaries* all around the surviving portions of the heart, in order to supply oxygen and nutrients at levels previously not enjoyed by this damaged organ. In addition, all the other benefits accrue to the heart-attack survivor to such an extent that within a couple of years, the heart and its cardiovascular system are often stronger than they were prior to the attack, despite the "dead" cluster of cells.

And, if you want to talk to a person truly motivated to do CV Renewal, just spend 15 minutes with a heart-attack survivor. It's an unforgettable experience.

I've noted that excess LDL cholesterol and insufficient HDL cholesterol contribute to the plaque build-up that precipitates heart attacks. And you've already read in this chapter about the effects of CV Renewal on HDL: that number will rise in response to CV renewal activity.

What about LDL? What will drive that number down? It is clear that LDL responds dramatically and quickly to nutritional changes. It is also clear that LDL drops NOT in response to eating low amounts of cholesterol in food. Purchasing "low cholesterol" foods in the grocery store is a false strategy. The issue is the fat content of food – not the cholesterol content of food.

Your body manufactures cholesterol. It needs a certain amount. It does not convert the cholesterol you eat into more cholesterol. It converts the fat you eat into excess cholesterol. Fruits and vegetables have no fat. Animal muscle does.

To get the best anti-heart-disease package available, combine CV Renewal activity with a low-fat approach to eating (and, of course, with a program to stop smoking if you have that addiction). Couple that with the kinds of stress-shaping activities I've suggested in the previous chapters. *That* is a package you can live with.

I don't want to leave you with the impression that I have remained as stupid as I was that day so long ago when I zoomed past Kris as she picked that flower. And, I'm thankful to say, I didn't have to survive a heart attack to get my attitude adjusted.

Like a lot of sports-soaked athletes, though, I had to be *humbled* into an acceptance of CV Renewal as a concept. You may remember my saying that I bade goodbye to my faculty basketball colleagues for the (self-predicted) three months that I'd take to prepare for and run the Canadian National Capital Marathon. And you may remember my deciding to start with five-mile runs, and to build up every day until I could run the 26.2 miles that every marathon requires. And you may also remember that I launched those first daily runs at a speed just under my sprinting speed.

Obviously I got hurt. And that made me mad. How could I be hurt? No one was tackling me. No one was swinging a lacrosse stick at me. No one was elbowing me under the boards. How could I be hurt? So, with each "overuse injury" (the term for repetition injuries), I'd disgustedly take a day off, then return with renewed fury to my running.

I'll spare you further detail in this saga of psychological combat with a marathon obsession, and go to the happy ending. One pleasantly warm mid-summer day in upstate New York, having not run (again) because of pain from an overuse injury in my knees, or hips, or ankle, I decided not to run, but to walk over to the university's baseball fields and do some reading.

I arrived at the baseball complex, which was deserted, took off my shoes, put my book and notepad down on the grass, and started to ... er ... "jog" through the outfield expanse. I wasn't running. I was sort of walking/jogging. My rate of travel was considerably slower than I could have walked, had I been striding at my normal crossing-the-campus pace.

The outfields were bordered by stands of trees and shrubs. I noticed them. In those stands of vegetation, there was small wildlife. I noticed. On the outfield grass itself, there were butterflies and the occasional industrious bee. I noticed them, too.

I also noticed eventually that I wasn't out of breath, that I wasn't perspiring, and that ... incredibly ... I was not counting the seconds until I could stop. I was ... well ... enjoying this.

Furthermore, I wasn't hurting myself physically. And mentally, I was able to shift gears into a planning mode whenever I wished – which, for me, is often. And when I finally decided to stop, I felt no fatigue whatsoever. In fact, I felt refreshed. I felt *renewed.*

Section IV:
Renewal and Recommitment

Chapter 12

The Real World: You, Your Colleagues, and Your Administration

We've covered a lot of territory since Chapter 1 – "Pudding and Prime Movers." Let's take a look at putting this into a package.

I have emphasized approaches you can take to your personal/professional renewal without needing to rely on other people: administrators, colleagues, family members. I want you to think almost entirely in terms of renewal elements that you can design and control yourself.

That way, you remain self-reliant. And that way, you maintain a position of psychological control over your renewal process (and thus, you keep yourself at the "learned optimism" end of the Seligman continuum, consistently sensing connections between your efforts and the outcomes of your efforts).

As we've discussed, this "learned optimism" orientation promotes enhanced persistence and reduced stress as you move through your self-designed, self-implemented Professional Development Plan.

Contracts, Pair-tracts, and Tri-tracts

Hardly anyone can execute something as long-running as a Professional Development Plan without writing something down. Throughout this book, I provide sample worksheets and blank worksheets. Use them, and the checklist I'll give you in this final chapter, as your framework.

Near the end of Chapter 5, I gave you the most extensive set of worksheets in the book. And at the conclusion of that sequence, I provided space in which you were encouraged to write the elements in your Professional Development Plan. If you followed the format there, you wrote a series of action steps for yourself, both short- and long-term.

Think of those action steps in your Professional Development Plan as a ***self-contract.*** This becomes an agreement you make with yourself. Make it as formal as you like. Some teachers choose to write down those action steps, label those pages a "self-contract," and then sign and actually have the document witnessed.

Witnessed! Does that seem stupid? Not if it fosters the implementation of your Professional Development Plan. If it does that, it could be one of the smartest things you've ever done. But who would take seriously the witnessing of such a non-legal document?

I'll tell you who would. Another teacher.

- Find another teacher who has read *High-Energy Teaching*. Maybe on your own faculty; maybe on another school's faculty; maybe your former college roommate who lives 2,000 miles away. Doesn't matter.

- Don't just stop with asking that person to witness the "self-contract edition" of your Professional Development Plan. Do a **pair-tract** with that person. "Witness" each other's self-contract, *and then set up a schedule that calls for mutual submission of each self-contract to the witnessing professional.*

- The two of you can arrange to meet at the end of each month (or, if it's the 2,000-miles-away former roommate, arrange to fax-and-phone at the end of each month). Report to each other on your progress, on your barriers, and on your successful or unsuccessful efforts to overcome the barriers.

- If your pair-tract partner is on your own faculty, as will certainly be the case in many instances, be careful. Don't let these monthly pair-tract reports become complaint sessions. You can do that in the faculty lounge any time you feel you must. Stick to the purpose: a friendly-but-professional reporting to a colleague about your

Professional Development Plan efforts, successes, and non-successes since you last met.

- Make your monthly pair-tract session part of a Brown Bag Breakfast or Brown Bag Lunch or Brown Bag After-school Snack (BBASS). I recommend the BBASS to you. Pair-tract participants tend to enjoy that most, and profit from it most, because they feel more free to concentrate on the pair-tract. No imminent classes to teach, parents to see, meetings to chair.

Could three colleagues do a pair-tract? Sure. That becomes a tri-tract. Tri-tracts work fine. But after that, expect diminishing returns from the further addition of colleagues to your pair-tract or tri-tract system. Groups of four, five, six, and more usually become too unwieldy to meet the essential goal of this collegial arrangement: careful, thoughtful examination of individual progress on your Professional Development Plans.

Larger groups than three can serve other purposes nicely. But in my experience, such groups take away the privacy necessary for honest, useful, unself-conscious examination of pair-tracts with one or two colleagues.

SO, SHOULD YOU DO YOUR PROFESSIONAL DEVELOPMENT PLAN ALONE OR NOT? I can't answer that for you, but I can say this. Throughout *High-Energy Teaching,* I've emphasized the importance of your proceeding *alone* on your self-renewal path. I base my position on years of observation of faculties in motion. When individual teachers assume that they *must* be part of a group – whether it is a small, grade-level or department-level group, a whole-faculty system, and/or an administration-designed, administration-led, semi-coercive professional development effort – not much tends to happen.

In my experience, the most successfully self-renewing teachers tend to operate alone, *but with an obvious willingness to be inclusive when colleagues (either on the same faculty or from other faculties, as is the case often with professional associations) show an interest in that individual's efforts.*

They tend to prefer to write their own Professional Development Plan, and to incorporate a review of that Plan in their version of the once-monthly Ritual Reflection session.

I just wrote, "The most successfully self-renewing teachers *tend* to operate alone." Remember that the solo-versus-partner(s) question does not have to be all-or-nothing. For example, you could operate solo, just with your self-contract, much of the year, but set up a pair-tract with a colleague for mutual review of your self-contracts once a semester or once a year.

Or you could just decide that, for any number of good reasons – an especially good friend on your faculty, an especially valuable mentor on your faculty, or your own preference for teaming anything that can reasonably be teamed – you prefer the pair-tract or tri-tract arrangement to operating alone.

That really does NOT matter. What matters is that you do it.

Faculty Evaluation Systems Versus Your Individual Professional Development Plan

Those two things do not go together well. The administrator's faculty evaluation system has as its main purpose the evaluation of the faculty. Thus its name: faculty evaluation system.

Your individual Professional Development Plan has as its main purpose your continual personal/professional self-renewal. Thus its name: Your Professional Development Plan.

What if you have an administrator who (like me, when I was one) wants both things to happen at the same time, and within the same "system"? What should you do about that?

Stop her! That's what. It can't be done.

But there is a way for that administrator to proceed. She can, with the faculty's collective and individual help, establish *parallel tracks* for the two systems.

This can work especially well if the administrator is willing to set up the faculty evaluation system (**not** to be confused with the Professional Development Plans for faculty renewal) as follows:

- annual (summer) meetings with each teacher, during which the teacher and the administrator work out a set of objectives for the coming year for that teacher;

- the annual meeting characterized by the *teacher* proposing three to five major personal/professional objectives for herself/himself, while the administrator responds with one or two major personal/professional objectives for that teacher, followed by a combining of the two lists, with consent as mutual as possible;
- the cooperative (teacher with administrator) construction of a simple, informal "research design" to answer the question that must be asked overtly or implicitly of the teacher by the administrator, "How will I know you've made progress during the year toward your objectives?"
- implementation of this informal research design, which, depending upon the mutually agreed-upon objectives, may include such things as the submission of a written report by the teacher, a parent survey by the teacher, some classroom observations by the administrator, classroom observations by a colleague, an oral report by the teacher to the faculty, etc.;
- periodic meetings (quarterly? once a semester?) between the teacher and the administrator, during which the original objectives are re-examined by both the administrator and the teacher, discussed in depth, modified if appropriate, and extended;
- a final "closure meeting" at the end of the year, reviewing progress and discussing tentatively the upcoming year's objectives.

When I present that list of ideas for the evaluation process to administrators, I get a question: "Will that kind of documentation hold up if I have to fire a teacher?"

My answer to that is "Probably." The issue in firing is due process. There should be evidence that efforts were made to improve the unsatisfactory aspects of performance, and that clear warnings were delivered to the teacher that, without improvement on the teacher's part, a new contract might not be issued. If the faculty evaluation system is done well, it can serve many purposes, including that one.

The next question from administrators is a happier one: "How should that kind of administrative evaluation of faculty system fit with the kind of Professional Development Plan for individual self-renewal system advocated by *High-Energy Teaching*?

Well, the two systems "fit" by leaving each other ALONE. By staying "parallel." By making sure that administrators do not let their "evaluation" systems encroach on the teachers' "renewal" systems.

To be explicit: Communication between these two systems should be either non-existent or one-way, *at the individual teacher's discretion*. If a teacher decides, in a quarterly update meeting with his administrator (for the purpose of reviewing his progress on his evaluation-system objectives), to disclose some of what he has accomplished in working on his Professional Development Plan – his self-renewal self-contract – he *may*. If an administrator decides, in the same meeting, that she'd like to inquire about the teacher's progress in working on his Professional Development Plan – his self-renewal self-contract – she *may not*.

The faculty's self-renewal system is systemically fragile. Individual self-contracts or pair-tracts or tri-tracts are wonderful vehicles for renewal. But these Professional Development Plans will shatter in an instant if they are co-opted by well-intentioned administrators like me, who honestly do want faculty renewal above all things, but who think that, if they're just smart enough, they can devise a faculty evaluation system that fosters teacher renewal.

It won't work. It can't work. The desire for teacher renewal must come first from the individual *teacher*. That's not to say, though, that good administrators – and there are certainly many – cannot facilitate the faculty's self-renewal efforts. This can be done, and it is a delightful thing to find wherever it exists.

For example, if you, a fifth-grade teacher, devise a Professional Development Plan that calls for things such as:

- occasional observation – maybe three times, this year – of a master teacher's classroom, for a half-hour each time; or,
- enrollment as an auditor in a nearby university, in a course taught by a professor known for her ability to inspire, motivate, and communicate to students the most current research-based ideas for elementary/middle-school social studies teaching; or,

- the purchase and study of a series of three recent books on developmental reading theory and practice for underachievers; or,
- the purchase and review of a videotape depicting supportive class control approaches with middle-school students; or,
- a one-time trip to another school in your metropolitan area for a day of observing its use of instructional software with fifth grade students ...

THEN you have an excellent set of reasons to ask for a meeting with the appropriate administrator, to outline the relevant portions of your Professional Development Plan for her, and to request formally her support in your efforts. In the examples just given, that support might take the form of helping with arrangements to cover your classes when you observe elsewhere, or providing financial support for auditing the university class or purchasing books or tapes.

That's how administrators can support faculty self-renewal – by calling the faculty's attention to these self-renewal ideas, by encouraging the teachers to investigate the ideas and then to implement them, by being positively reinforcing to any efforts on the part of teachers to formulate and pursue their own Professional Development Plans, and by responding as positively as possible to the resulting requests from teachers, if any, of the sort I just listed. But NOT by incorporating the faculty's self-renewal processes into the administration's faculty evaluation system.

Fragments or Wholeness?

Near the end of Chapter 5, I gave you a framework for your Professional Development Plan. Consider using the summary chart on the next two pages as a concise review sheet for both the process and the content of your Plan.

Your Professional Development Plan: Review of Ingredients

This checklist is designed for use in any of five settings:

1. your private, monthly, Ritual Reflection sessions;
2. your private, regular – perhaps monthly – reviews of your progress in your Professional Development Plan;
3. your actual drafting of your Professional Development Plan, both the initial writing and any subsequent rewrites through the months and years;
4. your discussions with colleagues, should you enter into a pair-tract or tri-tract arrangement; and/or,
5. your discussions with an administrator, should you choose to communicate portions of your Professional Development Plan to your administration.

		Item to implement	In occasional use	In regular use
1.	Prime Movers/First Purposes review (Chapter 9: Ritual Reflection Chart I)	☐	☐	☐
2.	Habituated Thoughts review (Chapter 9: Ritual Reflection Chart II)	☐	☐	☐
3.	Habituated Thoughts log sheet (Chapter 9: Ritual Reflection Chart II: Habituated Thoughts)	☐	☐	☐
*4.	Ritual Reflection: monthly utilization (Chapter 9)	☐	☐	☐
5.	"Off-center Leadership" approaches and techniques (Chapter 4)	☐	☐	☐
6.	Classroom approaches/ techniques (Chapters 4, 6)**	☐	☐	☐

	Item to implement	In occasional use	In regular use
*7. Professional Development Plan			
Review of Assumptions (Chapter 5)	☐	☐	☐
Development of Framework (Chapter 5)	☐	☐	☐
Development of Outline (Chapter 5)	☐	☐	☐
8. Stress Shaping			
Stressor Calendar (Chapter 8)	☐	☐	☐
Cognitive Habits (Chapter 9)	☐	☐	☐
In-Action Stress Shaping (Chapter 10)	☐	☐	☐
CV Renewal (Chapter 11)	☐	☐	☐
9. Solo/team Considerations			
Pair-tracts, tri-tracts (Chapter 12)	☐	☐	☐
Administrative involvement (Chapter 12)	☐	☐	☐

*OF GREATEST IMPORTANCE

** See also, *Twenty Principles for Teaching Excellence: The Teacher's Workbook*.

Of the several elements in the two-page checklist most likely to be forgotten or ignored, the Stressor Calendar ranks high.

Don't. The Stressor Calendar provides one of the best means available to help you *integrate* your life components meaningfully. Because the Stressor Calendar chapter leads you to consider all your "obligations" systematically, and because it forces you to categorize and calculate the pressures you face, it is an important tool for every busy person. Often, a teacher's use of the Stressor Calendar will lead her to reevaluate time and energy commitments in significant ways, and to prioritize *usefully* for the first time in years. The more you can integrate your Professional Development Plan's components with each other and with the rest of your "life commitments," the better.

You may remember reading in an earlier chapter about my arrival at St. Lawrence University in the early '70s, and my initial astonishment at the "freedom" of my days. I have one more word for you about that first year.

Upon completion of the spring semester, my department chair set up a meeting with me to do an "individual faculty evaluation." I appeared dutifully at the scheduled time, and together he and I went through a series of printed, evaluative criteria he supplied. We considered each item on this instrument, and we discussed my performance and agreed upon a number – a point on a continuum – to represent the quality of my performance on that aspect of my first-year professorship.

The session went fine. But I was struck by the emptiness and – to use the phrase I would now use – by the sense of *learned helplessness* I experienced in the meeting's aftermath.

My department chair's criteria/continua comprised "traits," such as dependability, creativity, ability to work with groups (such as my colleagues, and others). I was pleased that he and I agreed that I should have high scores on most of the items. His system seemed to me a good one for faculty *evaluation*.

But my internal response to the event stemmed from, as I would now say, my sense of *an absence of clear connections between my year-long efforts, as a beginning college professor, and the (perceived) outcomes of those efforts*. The tie-in of his evaluation instrument to my actual, real-life, concentrated efforts to teach well, to research well, to counsel well, and to administrate well were too tenuous to reinforce me positively. It was a depressing experience, a fact which would no doubt have surprised my department chair. After all, hadn't we agreed that I'd done well?

A teaching unit I often used in those days was one – for school administrators – we called Management-by-Objectives (MBO). During the summer following my department chair's evaluation session with me, I thought about Dr. Peter Drucker's writings on Management-by-Objectives, and about my evaluation meeting, and about how I felt about that good-but-depressing evaluation experience.

When we began the next school year, I wrote a four-page document in which I spelled out the *explicit* goals, objectives, and targets I wanted to set for myself that year. I showed the document to my department chair, and asked that it be used as a supplementary "evaluation" instrument for me, in combination with his existing instrument.

He was a good sport about it.

So, at the end of my second year, he and I reviewed both instruments. I talked him through every aspect of my self-reported and self-analyzed MBO instrument.

He liked it. He felt that he knew much more about what I'd worked on that year than he had the year before, and *I felt clear connections between my efforts and the (newly perceived) outcomes of my efforts.*

Today, I'd call that a learned-optimistic evaluation event.

But was my MBO document really "faculty evaluation"? Or was it what I now call "faculty self-renewal"? Well, I'd say now that it was faculty self-renewal. It *became* evaluation because I chose to tell my department chair about it. And he was glad to hear it. And he chose to incorporate what I told him, and the data I supplied him, in his evaluation of me.

Even though at that time I would have understood only a little about what I have now written in *High-Energy Teaching*, I had accidentally stumbled onto a sound process. I now view that process, in retrospect, as a rudimentary-but-successful model for the kinds of things teachers can do on their own to foster professional development, and which can, given a willing administrator, be fit onto a parallel track with conventional evaluation systems to give both administrators and teachers what they want and need.

One Man's Life: Sustainable Losses and the Common Good

Writer Kenny Moore wrote of the late Arthur Ashe that Ashe had "signed his contract with the whole society of man." Ashe had insisted, wrote Moore, that there are only two alternatives. "If enough human beings do not advance the common good, we cannot go on; we shall move from suffering a chain of sustainable losses to suffering extinction."[1]

I won't assume that you know who Arthur Ashe was. I will tell you that he was a man who was once among the best tennis players in the world, but a man who had long since transcended sports to become a quiet, *commanding* spokesperson for, in Moore's words, "whatever mends and perpetuates the widest community, whether it is a student's decision to set worthy goals, a gene-splicing technique to combat HIV, or a South African election open to members of all races."

Within weeks of the interview from which Moore's words were drawn, Arthur Ashe was dead of AIDS-related causes. He had contracted the virus years before, from a blood transfusion during surgery.

From surgery! How utterly unfair, said some.

Not Ashe: "No, my faith hasn't been shaken .... These things just happen. Earthquakes, storms, innocent people get killed. But it does shake one's faith in the *causality* between good works and just rewards."

You are a teacher. There are days when you see little connection between your good works – your efforts to teach young people, and to lead them into a greater understanding of life – and the outcomes of your efforts. At those times, it is hard to think in high-minded terms.

---

1 Reprinted courtesy of *Sports Illustrated* from the December 21, 1992 issue. © 1992, Time, Inc. ("The Eternal Example" by Kenny Moore.) All Rights Reserved.
Ashe, still living at the time, was honored as Sportsman of the Year.

But you must. Above all professions, teaching is the highest-minded. And thus, it should take its proper place, with marriage, with our parenting commitments, with our religious commitments, in Ritual Reflection, and ritual recommitment to its fundamental meaning: "... Whatever mends and perpetuates the widest community ...."

The sense of community you create in your classroom represents exactly what humankind must do now. And better than before.

Teaching cannot, and must not, be viewed by its practitioners as anything less than the heart of this society's sense of community. Because if it is allowed to become less than that, then there can be nothing sacred (secular or religious) about *meaningful* life. Teaching is the profession that, in American society, endeavors to provide *meaningful*, self-responsible, communally responsible life, above all other professions.

Those phrases associated with Ashe – "a contract with the whole society of man," "the advance of the common good," "the uncertain causality between good works and just rewards" – apply here. When I spoke in an earlier chapter of the heroism of a young woman in her first year of teaching, I spoke of you, too. Every day you spend in this contract with the whole society, advancing the common good, fighting to establish a sense of causality between your efforts and those efforts' outcomes, working to give your students that same sense of causality between their efforts and their efforts' outcomes – every day you do these things, you behave in ways justly called heroic.

Said Ashe, "Each of us comes up with his or her own social contracts, agreements with our group or our nation, or just ourselves." Your career and its implied commitments represent the epitome of the *meaning-filled* social contract in our society. On behalf of all of those who parent children, all of those who work for the good of this society, all of those who wish for this society's health, now and in the longest-term future – I salute you.

Section V:
Appendix

Appendix

An Overview of the Center for Teacher Renewal International Model Schools Project

This overview is in no sense a "final report," as the project is designed to be ongoing indefinitely. While the composition of the schools in the study will continue to change regularly, the CTR expects to continue the project, using these general methods and assumptions, for years to come.

Background: An Earlier Case Study

Two members of the Yale University Department of Administrative Science conducted a four-year case study of a nearby high school during the early '70s. In this remarkable case study, the researchers examined the stresses, tensions, and resistance to change within the school's faculty and student cultures, paying special attention to how those variables fluctuated during each of the four school years studied.

The authors noted: "As the school year passed apathy and alienation increased; it was common for activities (such as the faculty forum), begun in the fall, to falter as the oppressive winter term set in."[1] This tendency for teacher/student "mood" to shift in patterned ways reasserted itself during each year of the study.

---

1 Alderfer, C. P., & Brown, L. D. *Learning from Changing: Organizational Diagnosis and Development,* Beverly Hills & London: Sage Publications, 1975, page 54.

Additional Background: The CTR Pilot Study of 1989

Interviews with leaders of 42 schools in 1989 provided basic information on the relationships to be studied. The hypotheses underlying the pilot were:

1. Student performance fluctuates predictably during the course of a given school year in many schools (in all grade levels), starting at high levels and declining throughout the year, in patterns reminiscent of those found in the Yale University study just noted.
2. Student stress varies inversely with student performance.
3. Student satisfaction fluctuates in patterns similar to those of student performance.
4. Teacher performance, stress, and satisfaction fluctuate in patterns similar to those found in the students.
5. Administrative performance, stress, and satisfaction fluctuate in patterns similar to those found in the students and teachers.

In structured interviews with leaders of 42 schools of many types, hypotheses #1, #2, and #3, above, were generally supported. Hypothesis #4 was supported in part. Hypothesis #5 was not supported.

A cluster of variables appeared to enhance the shapes of the annual patterns of student and faculty performance, stress, and satisfaction. The cluster was labeled the Affective Climate Enhancers (ACE). This cluster of items, which appeared in this descriptive study to help encourage year-round performance while reducing stress, included these:

1. programs fostering a sense of "community" within the school;
2. school-wide emphasis upon academic excellence;
3. high expectations of all students by all personnel;
4. student "responsibility" taught systematically;
5. required life skills and/or ethical decision-making courses;
6. systematic attention to matching students with the most appropriate learning environments/teachers;

7. the hiring and/or the development of "nurturing" faculty members in the high school as well as at the lower grade levels;
8. systematic networking (of student groups) with the community outside the school.

Pearson Product-Moment Correlations pairing the ACE cluster with the variables implied by the original hypotheses yielded these results:

Variables*	Coefficient	t-value	Significance
Student stress with ACE cluster	-.72	7.55(df=53)	<.001
Student performance with ACE cluster	+.31	2.41(df=53)	<.02
Student enthusiasm with ACE cluster	+.32	2.52(df=53)	<.02
Faculty performance with ACE cluster	+.29	2.24(df=53)	<.05
Faculty enthusiasm with ACE cluster	+.31	2.37(df=53)	<.05
Faculty stress with ACE cluster	-.14	1.05(df=53)	NS

* N=55 (Multi-unit schools' data have been tabulated as more than one school unit)

Curves plotted on each dimension showed that, with the exception of "faculty stress" (non-significant in its relationship to the ACE cluster, as shown by the table above), the general patterns of both student and faculty movement during a school year were strikingly similar to those shown by the previously noted Yale study.

Of particular interest in this pilot study was the finding that those schools that appeared most resistant to the Selye-Snelling Performance/Stress Curves did not treat "academic excellence" and "nurturing climate" as competing factors, but as complementary. Schools (of all grade levels) that were resistant to annual deterioration in performance offered students a challenging-but-safe academic experience. Nurturance for accelerated learning was the motif.

The Current Study

The 1989 pilot/descriptive study just summarized has been followed in subsequent academic years by a coordinated, multi-school case study focused on some of the statistically significant variables emerging from the pilot. These variables center on student performance, student stress, and the administrative and instructional factors appearing to influence within-year fluctuations in both student performance and student stress.

Nine schools were originally selected in order to provide the study with a varied sampling of school types. The original nine schools provided diversity in: administrative size and structure, faculty size, student-body size, grade levels of student body, metropolitan/rural location, and demographics of student body. CTR data collectors went on-site four times a year, usually during the week after the end of each grading period. The purpose of this timing was to correlate interview-derived data with performance data (grades or mid-period written reports).

At each of the original nine schools, 16 students (selected by stratified random methods in order to provide the full range of academic accomplishment) were interviewed during each on-site visit (the same 16 students each time), and their grades for the just-ended period were collected.

The youngest students interviewed were third-graders. Their inability to speak precisely about time frames for past and future events made some of their data suspect. Fifth-graders (and above) had few problems of that sort. The full range of grade levels that were eventually fitted to the study includes grades 3-13. (Canadian schools include grade 13.)

Students' grade levels (those selected for interviews) at each school varied. The CTR's typical pattern was to interview eight students at a low grade level (within the grade ranges offered by a particular school unit), and eight students at the second-highest grade level offered by a given school (e.g., the seventh grade in a middle school, or the 11th grade in a high school).

The Descriptive Study Process and Findings

Findings concerning teaching emerged from the following process:

1. In the structured interview settings, students described to CTR data collectors the kind and extent of "pressures" they felt during the preceding eight weeks of school.
2. They also provided their assessments of such factors as their teachers' perceived fairness in grading, their teachers' perceived efforts to help them do well, and the fairness of the amount of work they were asked to do (with "fairness" being defined as the optimum amount of work needed to prepare them for success at the next level of school).
3. Data were translated into interval data.
4. At the end of each school year, the grades of the 16 students (at each school) were plotted.
5. Schools were (confidentially) ranked according to their students' collective academic profiles (i.e., profiles developed from the consistency and/or fluctuation in the students' performance [grades]).
6. Schools in which the students' grades indicated consistently high student performance throughout the school year were placed high in this confidential ranking system; schools in which the students' grades deteriorated throughout the year were placed low in this ranking system; schools in which the students' grades followed erratic patterns throughout the school year were placed mid-range in this ranking system.
7. When grades and stress levels (the latter inferred from the interview-based data translation process) were plotted together for all 144 students at the original nine schools, an inverse relationship between the two patterns — student performance and student stress — was apparent.
8. Schools in which student stress levels started high and continued high throughout the school year tended to display declining student performance profiles.

9. Schools in which student stress levels started mid-range and continued mid-range throughout the school year tended to display stable, high-level student performance profiles.
10. Schools in which student stress levels fluctuated throughout the school year tended to display fluctuating student performance profiles, and tended to display inverse relationships between the two (stress and performance).
11. Using the ranking system described in #6, above, a model for teacher attitudes/behaviors was constructed; teacher attitudes/behaviors associated most prominently with the higher ranking schools (especially when those attitudes/behaviors were only minimally present or even absent in lower ranking schools) formed the core of the model's descriptors.
12. The model resulting – for teacher attitude/behavior – is delineated at length throughout the book *Twenty Principles for Teaching Excellence: The Teacher's Workbook*, and is both assumed and discussed explicitly in this volume, *High-Energy Teaching*.

Additional Comments

Two of the more striking in-process outcomes of the study were these:

(a) Students' views of their teachers tended to be consistent within a given school, regardless of whether or not a particular student was academically doing well or doing poorly (e.g., in higher-ranked schools, even marginal students tended to assert that teachers were fair and that teachers extended themselves forcefully and even heroically in their efforts to move all students toward academic success; conversely, in lower-ranked schools, even superior students decried the lack of fairness in their teachers and stated consistently that their academic achievements were attained despite their teachers).

(b) In higher-ranked schools, students viewed their teachers as interested, academically excited, still engaged themselves in their own learning processes ("professional development"), demanding and "on their side," and "persistently wishing them the best" (and yet not willing mere-

merely to give students good marks in the absence of students' efforts to achieve them). There was, in short, a "faculty culture" which students understood very well, although they almost never overtly analyzed it.

The psychological/conceptual framework for the study was derived in part from the work of Dr. Martin E. P. Seligman at the University of Pennsylvania. His development of the concepts of "learned helplessness" and of "learned optimism" undergird the student interview format and procedure, and, as well, the data translation process.[2]

"Learned helplessness," as utilized conceptually in this study, tends to result from experiences in which an individual cannot find connections between her or his efforts – and those efforts' perceived outcomes. (Note that a "bad" or "non-existent" student effort should, in this framework, receive negative, or perhaps no, reinforcement from the teacher. Providing positive reinforcement for poor student effort reinforces learned helplessness just as does the absence of positive reinforcement in response to high levels of student effort and excellence.)

Countervailing teacher behaviors include: providing clear structure for students' efforts (frameworks outlining potential success trails), maintaining high expectations for all students (but adapting those expectations to individuals' abilities), persisting every day in helping all students to reach those high expectations, and distributing psychological reinforcement quickly, unremittingly, and with precision.

Twenty Principles for Teaching Excellence: The Teacher's Workbook and this companion piece, *High-Energy Teaching,* are the result of finding that these learned-helplessness/learned-optimism concepts were associated with high, declining, or erratic student performance patterns, depending in each case upon the extent to which either learned helplessness or learned optimism prevailed within a given faculty/student environment. The phrase "high stress" was applied to student responses generally associated with learned-helpless behavior; "moderate stress," with learned-optimistic behavior.

---

2 For more on the ideas that undergird these formulations, see Seligman's outstanding volume, *Learned Optimism,* New York: Knopf, 1991; and *Psychopathology: Experimental Models,* San Francisco: Freeman, 1977.

Index

CTR™

ism Center for Teacher Renewal™

The ISM Center for Teacher Renewal (CTR) enhances student performance by providing programs and support for teachers as they work on their professional development plans for improved classroom performance and personal renewal.

To achieve this, the CTR engages in primary and custom-designed research, publishes books and periodicals, conducts workshops, and provides speakers and consulting services to schools, associations, and corporations interested in student performance and teacher renewal.

High-Energy Teaching is the second book produced by the CTR for use by teachers in the formulation of a plan for lifetime career growth and satisfaction. The first book, *Twenty Principles for Teaching Excellence*, was published in 1992 as the result of CTR's research into student and teacher performance and stress.

In response to the need for a systematic way to introduce the principles and encourage ongoing individual teacher renewal, CTR designed a Faculty Renewal Program, which includes:

- *High-Energy Teaching* and *Twenty Principles for Teaching Excellence* – complementary books that serve as the "course guide" to teacher renewal
- *Teachers in Touch* – a newsletter for professional sharing published five times during the school year
- *Teaching From the Inside Out* – an Introductory presentation on videotape – by M. Walker Buckalew
- A 10-Step Implementation Guide – a facilitator's plan for putting the CTR Faculty Renewal Program into action

For additional information on the ISM Center for Teacher Renewal and its products and services, write to:

ISM Center for Teacher Renewal
1316 North Union Street
Wilmington, Delaware 19806-2594
Or call
1-800-955-4944